WALKS
in Coquetdale

A guide to eleven walks
of between five and thirteen kilometres in length
in and around the Northumberland National Park
and one linear river walk of twenty two kilometres.

Produced and published by
Northumberland County Council
National Park and Countryside Department
Eastburn, South Park, Hexham, Northumberland.

Text by Joan Williams
Edited by Caroline Freeman
Photographs by Karen Melvin and Andrew Miller
Designed and illustrated by Brian Waters

ISBN 0 907632 14 9

Typesetting by Reed Typesetting, North Shields, Tyne and Wear.
Printed by Wards (Colour Printers), Dunston, Gateshead, Tyne and Wear.

Contents

WITH FIFTEEN 1:25000 MAPS

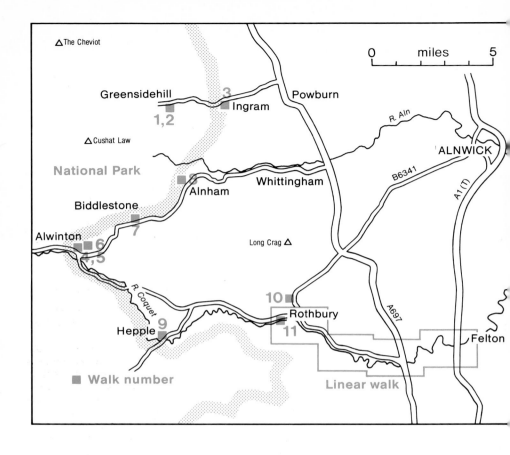

Follow the
Country Code

**Enjoy the countryside
and respect its life and work
Guard against all risk of fire
Fasten all gates
Keep your dogs under close control
Keep to public paths across farmland
Use gates and stiles
to cross fences, hedges and walls
Leave livestock, crops and machinery alone
Take your litter home
Help to keep all water clean
Protect wildlife, plants and trees
Take special care on country roads
Make no unnecessary noise**

Introduction

THE NORTHUMBERLAND NATIONAL PARK is one of ten National Parks in England and Wales. It is not the largest but within its elongated shape it contains as much, if not more variety of scenery as the larger National Parks.

It is the quality and variety of scenery within the Park that attracts so many walkers and enables visitors to feel a sense both of adventure and of solitude.

The Northumberland National Park Authority is unique in having countryside functions extending outside the Park boundaries. It can therefore help walkers to enjoy following paths outside as well as inside the Park. The combined work of the Authority's staff of National Park Wardens and Footpaths Officers has contributed largely to the walks described in this booklet being readily available.

The aim of this booklet is to provide both visitors and local people with walking routes that they can follow and with interesting information regarding things to see on the way. Whilst it is hoped that walkers will enjoy using the routes described it is also hoped that they will accept the responsibility that goes with using the countryside, and keep the Country Code. This means causing as little disturbance as possible to farm stock, keeping dogs under control, leaving gates as they find them and, of course, not leaving litter to mar the enjoyment of the next walker on the route.

Starting points and transport

There is adequate car parking space at the start of each walk. Sometimes it will be a formal parking area with a hard surface whilst at others it will be a wide enough road verge to accommodate one or two cars at a time.

The starting points at Rothbury, Felton, Pauperhaugh and Weldon Bridge are on regular bus routes. It is possible to reach the remaining points at Alwinton, Hepple, Ingram and Alnham by public transport, but these have an infrequent service only. We recommend that you obtain a copy of Northumberland Public Transport Guide, published by United Automobile Services in association with Northumberland County Council. This contains full timetable details and tourist information.

National Parks in England and Wales

Some misconceptions surround the term 'National Park' because the Parks are not state owned and neither can they be compared with city parks; they also differ from the wild game National Parks of other countries. The nation may not own them, nor do we have unlimited rights of access over them, but they are certainly nationally recognised as areas of the highest quality scenery in England and Wales.

National Parks in this country came about as a result of Parliament passing the 'National Parks and Access to the Countryside Act' in 1949. The Act did not apply to Scotland which is why we talk only about the National Parks of England and Wales.

Selected as some of the finest remaining remote and open countryside — moor, mountain, valley and seashore — ten National Parks were designated between 1951 and 1957. They exist to safeguard particularly fine landscape and to assist the public to enjoy beautiful countryside for the purpose of open air recreation.

It must be remembered, however, that although an area is designated a National Park, no additional rights of access are automatically bestowed on the visitor. Much of the land in the Northumberland National Park is privately owned, some by the Forestry Commission and some by the Ministry of Defence. So except where the National Park Authority makes special provision, the walker may only go by public rights of way, (i.e. minor roads, footpaths and bridleways) and even then, in the case of Ministry of Defence land, only when it is safe to do so — red flags usually denote areas where it is forbidden and dangerous to enter for the time being.

A National Park Authority has a duty to conserve the landscape of its Park and to promote opportunities for people to enjoy it, but, in the latter case, only when due consideration has been given to the interests of those who live and work in the countryside. After all, it is the past care and attention by generations of landowners and farmers that has been largely responsible for the attractiveness of today's National Park landscape.

A National Park cannot become a rural museum. Farming and forestry practices go on changing, and if the countryside, as the farmers' and foresters' workshop, is to continue to make its valuable contribution to the Country's economy, then the landscape will go on changing and evolving too. However, the National Park Authorities are also planning authorities, and as such have some measure of control over what changes come about in the countryside.

Northumberland National Park

Rights of way and using this booklet

Where hedges, walls and fences mark off land ownership or divide up individual farms, public rights of way make it possible to move across land, which is effectively the farmer's workplace, without interfering with the daily business of making his living.

Apart from public roads (not necessarily 'made up') there are two types of right of way: footpaths and bridleways. Footpaths are simply routes which can be followed on foot whilst bridleways, originally wide enough to accommodate a man leading a horse, may today be walked, or ridden on horseback or on pedal cycle.

As part of the programme involved in the production of this booklet all routes have been examined and signposts, stiles and way-marks provided where necessary. Occasionally a signposted or waymarked change in a section of the path may be encountered. Any alternative route of this kind is planned to cause the minimum of inconvenience to the walker and we ask for your co-operation in following it.

Interpretive notes are printed in the text in normal weight type, but to avoid confusion route directions are given in bold type whilst the letters '(R)' and '(L)' mean 'to the right' and 'to the left' respectively. Also, in the interests of clarity, only those rights of way which form the described routes are shown on the maps, which are all at 1:25000 (2½" to the mile) scale. The route symbols are as follows:

Footpath .... Bridleway _ _ _ _ _ _
Permissive path _._._._Road _____

The terms 'footpath' and 'bridleway' indicate statutory rights of way and 'permissive path' indicates parts of the routes which walkers are permitted to use by courtesy of the landowner but which have no legal status.

The letters 'GR' refer to the Ordnance Survey grid reference system, details of which are printed on each of their 1:50000 series maps.

Enjoy your walk

Comfort is essential to the enjoyment of any walk so wear comfortable sensible shoes or boots where a reading of the route notes might suggest it. Woollen socks, being more absorbent, are usually better to wear than those made from artificial fibres.

Walking may seem to be warm work but, especially at higher levels, it is possible to become chilled. Carry a pullover or jumper which can be put on if the temperature drops, and remember a waterproof will keep out the wind as well as keep off the rain.

A leisurely pace is a comfortable pace. Walks in this booklet have been calculated at roughly 2½ kilometres per hour to allow enough time for even the least experienced walker to complete the route.

3

Ingram

The valley of the River Beamish, which rises on the slopes of the Cheviot, tumbles at the foot of steep, over-shadowing hillsides and then flows placidly along a broadening valley, is the setting for this small village.

The National Park Authority, with the co-operation of local landowners has created a number of excellent riverside parking and picnic places, and there are toilet facilities.

There is much evidence of prehistoric life on the surrounding hills: hillforts, settlements and burial cairns. Evening sunlight shows up the lynchets, or terraces, of medieval ploughing running across the hillsides.

Not far from the bridge at the entrance to the village is a National Park Information Centre which has books, maps and souvenirs for sale, and refreshments for the hungry or thirsty walker.

There is no bus service, although Post Buses run at certain times.

South-east from Alnhammoor

1 Hartside-Alnhammoor-Little Dod; return via Low Bleakhope

11km, about 4½ hours. A long walk into a seldom visited and remote part of the hills, amidst the beautiful wild countryside of the upper Breamish. There are few clear paths across the hills, so it is advisable to wear walking boots or strong shoes.

Park 5km up the valley from Ingram on the left hand grass verge just before the sign to Alnhammoor (L) (GR 977162). Hartside Farm is just ahead, and no cars are permitted to drive beyond it, except ones going to the houses at Linhope. Walk along the road (L) signposted Alnhammoor.

You may see some rather strange looking four-horned sheep grazing beside the road. These are Jacobs. Some farmers like to mate the tups with the young ewes as the resultant lambs are small and finely boned and are born without much difficulty. The lambs are destined for the butcher, so their mixed parentage makes no difference and the meat is considered to be more lean and tender.

Jacob sheep derive their name from the passage in the Bible where Jacob says to Laban, 'I will pass through all thy flocks this day and separate from them all the sheep with little spots and great spots and all the black lambs among the sheep'. It has taken 400 years for this sheep to be recognised as a positive breed, and because of the Biblical mention the name Jacob was thought to be appropriate.

It is believed that the breed came originally from Palestine, moved along the north coast of Africa to Morocco and so over to Spain. Possibly, during the reign of Queen Elizabeth I the Spanish Armada carried them for use as food and when the ships were wrecked off the coast of Scotland some of the sheep reached the shore and survived. Very ancient Chinese pictures show spotted sheep in existence before Biblical times, so perhaps they travelled to the Middle East along the Silk Road. Others say they are descended from an extinct Hebridian breed, related to the Soay sheep of St. Kilda. Whatever the truth, they have romantic origins.

Continue along the road for 1km and cross the bridge.

The conical hill with the cairn on top is Hogdon Law.

Before the bridge was built there was a ford here, very tricky in times of floods; indeed floods washed away the first bridge, parts of which are still to be seen a few yards upstream. After heavy rain or snowfall the burns and rivers still flood, but drainage of the higher slopes has prevented the sudden surges of long ago. A terrific downpour in July 1893 scooped out enormous masses of peat from the slopes of Bloodybush Edge, a hill further up the Breamish Valley and sent a tremendous volume of water down the Breamish which washed away everything in its path.

Follow the road up through a gate (please shut it), pass a barn (L) and continue over the cattle grid.

This is the house of Alnhammoor, the first of three isolated shepherds' cottages linked by this road. It is because of this road that the cottages are still inhabited; many walks in this book pass cottages abandoned and derelict because they are accessible only by foot or on horseback.

Walk on for 50m and go through gate in the wall (L). Turn right to follow the wall (R) until a fence is reached. Turn left along the fence, over a stile and down to cross the Rowhope Burn by a plank bridge.

The Shank Burn, on the left, is draining the slopes of Hogdon Law. It joins the River Breamish just past Alnhammoor house.

Ring ouzel

5

Keeping the Shank Burn on your left walk 250m to a cairn, then straight on up the slope. At the top of the bank continue on up the slope to the gate seen in the middle of the fence on the skyline.

The granite tors of Great and Little Standrop are clearly seen if you pause for a backward look, and Hedgehope (714m), the second highest hill of the Cheviot Range rears behind them. In the foreground behind the trees is Ritto Hill, near Linhope Spout.

Go through the gate and follow the path straight on, uphill at first, to pass a sheep stell away to the left in 600m.

Shank House, another remote shepherd cottage is seen behind its shelter belt of trees (L). The road to it comes over the hills from Alnham, to the south-east. There were high jinks on those hills over a hundred years ago. On 28 December 1849 Joseph Turnbull of Netherton married Mary Amos of Shank House, at Alnham Church. This being the marriage of a son and daughter of two of the oldest families in the district, it was a great occasion. The bridal party accompanied by a fiddler playing tunes set out on foot from Shank House to the church, three miles over the hills. After the ceremony a party of about 60 people set out for the return journey. As soon as the hilltop was reached and they could see Shank House, the bride's mother appeared, waving a large, bright-coloured silk handkerchief. This was the prize for the first runner to reach the house, and the race was called 'The Running for the Kail'. Off the young men went, jumping the tussocks and floundering through the bogs. Getting hot, they threw off coats, hats, scarves, etc., which were gathered up by the laughing party in the rear. Jack of Linshiels won the Kail, and when everyone had reached the house there was a great feast and dancing afterwards which went on far into the night.

The path becomes less clear beyond the stell. Walk up the slope (cairned) with Scaud Knowe to your right, and when the view ahead opens up aim to the right of Little Dod — a low rounded hill seen down to the left.

The small hill is Little Dod. Many hills in

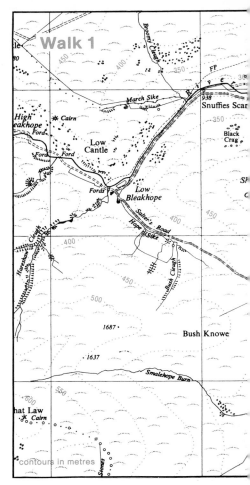

Northumberland are called Dod; the name means rounded. In the Scottish Borderlands polled cattle are called 'doddies'.

Looking ahead, south westwards, is a gash in the hillside, where the Sting Burn rises. Sting is said to be derived from an old word meaning a post, or pole, and apparently there was once a stone marker at the dip where Sting Burn flows down between Hogdon Law (L) and Cushat Law (R), at Sting Head. Cushat Law — cushat means wood pigeon —is the fourth highest hill in the Cheviot Range, at 616m.

Away to the left, beyond the Shank House plantation, the Salter's Road can be seen ascending the hill on its way to Alnham. This

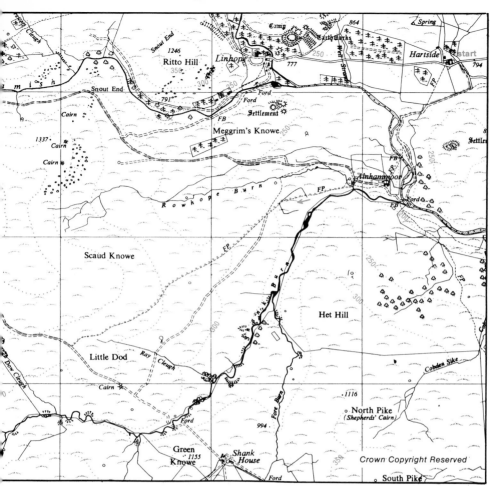

old track gets its name from the carrying, and indeed smuggling of salt by packhorse from the salt pans on the coast into Scotland, to avoid the payment of tax.

At the grassy patch by Little Dod, bear right at a cairn and follow the Salter's Road track (cairned) up and over the ridge to the gate.

Dow Cleugh, a small ravine, is to the left. You may be lucky and see a ring ouzel hereabouts. The male bird is black with a pronounced white crescent on its breast. Ring ouzels, also called mountain blackbirds, are summer visitors and breed on heathery scars like the ones at Dow Cleugh, at heights of over 300m.

Go through the gate, straight ahead across

200m of rough ground, then follow the Salter's Road down the valley to the farmhouse.

The valley below is that of the upper Breamish, and the farm is Low Bleakhope. High Bleakhope lies further up the valley. The pronunciation is 'Blake-up'. 'Bleak' means black or heather land and a 'hope' is a strip of fertile land in a valley.

The Salter's Road runs up the valley, passes High Bleakhope farmhouse, then bears left to cross the hills and meet up with Clennell Street, another old drove road, near Windy Gyle. The Salter's Road was a route into Scotland as far back as the 13th century, and many smugglers, Border Reivers, travellers

Wood pigeon

On the right are the slopes of Shill Moor. The stony hillside is an ideal habitat for another summer visitor, the wheatear. This bird flits about near the ground, the flash of its white rump betraying its presence. Wheatears make their nests in crevices among rocks or in old rabbit burrows.

Continue, still on the road, around Shill Moor.

The Breamish now makes one of its many loops and flows at the foot of Ritto Hill. Hidden behind the trees is Linhope, a small hamlet at the end of the road up the Breamish Valley.

The road passes a small plantation (L).

The reasonably low level land to the left is Meggrim's Knowe. A knowe, pronounced 'now', is a hillock, or lesser hill or moorland slope. There were once several settlements, possibly Romano-British, on Meggrim's Knowe. When Roman soldiers had more or less pacified the area, the local inhabitants found it safe to leave the hilltop forts and live lower down, nearer water and better pasturing for their cattle. They continued to live in areas alongside the Roman armies. 'Romano-British' is normally used to identify steadings, settlements etc, inhabited by the civilian population during the Roman occupation of Britain.

and drovers have passed this way through the centuries.

Cross the Hope Sike, turn right in front of the house and follow the road down right.

Low Cantle (L) drops precipitously to the River Breamish. Along its lower slopes is evidence of soil creep, seen as a number of small terraces formed by the slow downward movement of earth loosened by the action of rain and frost.

Follow the road uphill around Snout End.

Walk along to Alnhammoor house about 1km, and then retrace your steps to the starting point near Hartside.

Hartside Farm with Dunmoor Hill in background

2 Hartside-Alnhammoor-Cobden;
return via Chesters

7½km, about 3 hours. This is a very pleasant walk. A short easy uphill stretch, then across an almost level grassy expanse with good views of the hills. There are clear paths for most of the way.

Park 5km up the valley from Ingram on the left hand grass verge just before Hartside Farm and the turning (L) for Alnhammoor (GR 977162). Walk along the Alnhammoor road for 1km to a bridge over the River Breamish.

The farm just ahead of the parking place is Hartside, and no cars are allowed beyond it except those having business in the hamlet of Linhope, 1½km along the road.

By the banks of the River Breamish, near the bridge, grows monkey flower. This water loving plant, the seeds of which are said to resemble a grinning monkey's face, has showy yellow flowers blotched with red. The closely related blood-drop emlets has quite large red blotches on yellow petals. Both plants were introduced from the Americas as garden flowers, but they are now naturalised and are found in many waterside areas.

Walk across the bridge and follow the road for 100m before turning left to cross the grassy slope in front of the cottage to a gate in the wall. Go through the gate and turn left on a track, through a gate, then right by the bridge over the Shank Burn.

Here the Shank Burn meets the River Breamish. This quiet stretch of water lined with trees is a spot favoured by goosanders. These long-bodied rakish birds are larger than wild ducks, and in flight the white body and wings and green-black head are noticeable. The female has a crested, chestnut head. Goosanders nest in holes in trees or in the riverbank. They often swim under water, looking for fish, and they can stay beneath the surface for nearly two minutes without coming up. The birds have a finely serrated bill which enables them to hold a slippery fish with ease. There are brown trout in the Breamish.

Proceed to a gate (stile) and bear right across the field towards a gate seen on a

slope by some trees. Continue up the hillside on a track, past a stell (L).

Pignut, or 'earth-nut', grows here. As the name indicates, pigs like the chestnut flavoured tuberous rootstock. The plant belongs to the carrot family and bears white flowers in the form of an umbel in early summer, but because it is low-growing it is often overlooked.

Pass beside the old rowan tree (R) near the top of the slope.

That the wind whips across these hills is shown by the way the rowan is leaning. This tree, often called mountain ash although it has no affinity with the ash proper, bears a red berry much appreciated by finches and thrushes. The seeds pass unscathed through their digestive systems and thus the tree appears in unexpected places.

The name rowan derives from the Norse 'runa', a charm, and the tree has long been associated with witchcraft. In the north-east of Scotland during the latter half of the 18th century, Beltane (or Mayday) Fires were lit with much ceremony in a fertility ritual, and pieces of rowan tree were placed over the cowshed doors to ensure a good supply of milk and to stop the witches from stealing it or casting spells on the cattle.

Goosanders

Chewing a piece of 'flying rowan' was most effective against witches when one was out at night, and if a piece was cut on Ascension Day and placed over the door, the house was made safe. 'Flying rowans' are those which grow out of another tree, or a cleft in the rock; the seed would have been sown by birds but because the rowan was not rooted in the ground like other trees it seemed strange to people of long ago. 'Flying rowans' can be found today in old woodlands on the Cheviots.

Continue up the track to the right-hand corner of the plantation.

A glance back discloses Ritto Hill and to the right of it the large rocky tor of Great Standrop on the lower slopes of Hedgehope Hill. Some 380 million years ago Hedgehope and The Cheviot were the site of volcanoes, the lava flows from which formed the surrounding rolling hills. This lava cooled into a rock called andesite, the soils of which support grass and bracken. Later intrusions of granite under the volcanoes cooled into an acid rock which formed the highest summits. The high land attracts the highest rainfall, and, as the rainwater cannot easily soak into the granite, boggy ground is formed. This wet land prevents heather, bracken, mosses and grasses from decomposing properly, resulting in a thick covering of black peat. Much later, the hills were worn down by ice during the Ice Ages, but the hard granite offered greater resistance to the ice flow and in places appears as tors; thus Great Standrop.

Go over the stile by the gate beside the trees.

A few grassy hummocks are all that remain of the cottage of Cobden. On 12 June 1840 a very happy, noisy party, some on horseback, some on foot, rushed past Cobden. William Thompson had married Ann Taylor at Alnham Church, and the wedding party then scampered helter-skelter over the hills to the house at Alnhammoor. When they hove in sight, the folk at the house gave a resounding cheer, guns were fired and the collie dogs barked. For days beforehand there had been great activity in the kitchen, the results of which were enjoyed by everyone, and later there were sports, dancing and merrymaking which lasted far into the small hours of the next morning, so the local records say.

Walk up the slope following a sunken track

Alnhammoor Farm from Shank Burn bridge

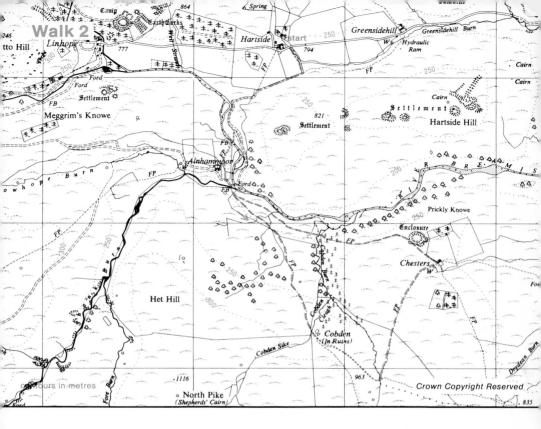

Walk 2

Crown Copyright Reserved

contours in metres

which soon levels out, until a ford is reached after ½km. Continue in the same line, ascending slightly for 100m to join a farm road.

This road, surfaced with the red felsite from the Harden Quarry at Biddlestone over the hills southwards, near Alwinton, was created to service the plantations and to facilitate the removal of the timber when the trees were felled.

At the road turn left and follow it to a gate. Continue towards the cottage of Chesters.

The jagged outline of Cunyan Crags is seen ahead, and to their left the land rises to the peaty hump of Dunmoor. In Old English 'dun' meant a hill. To the left again is the conical hill of Hedgehope. Still swinging to the left, one can see the long ridge of Shill Moor and another conical hill, Hogdon Law. 'Law' is derived from another Old English word 'hlaw' meaning hill. During the times of the Border

Troubles two men went up to the summit of Hogdon Law every day, to keep watch for marauding Scots.

The cottage of Chesters is now used by a scout troup as a centre for training in outdoor pursuits.

About 30m before the cottage turn up left and follow an indistinct path which passes just to the left of an ancient enclosure on the ridge top.

The circular grass-covered low wall enclosed a number of huts built during the time when the Romans occupied Britain. The huts were constructed of stone walls surmounted by a conical roof thatched with turf or heather. Wattle screens divided the interior into small rooms.

Follow the narrow path over the ridge to a wicket gate.

11

The river seen below later changes its name to the River Till. According to an old rhyme,

Foot of Breamish and head of Till,
Meet together at Berwick Hill.

Across the river are more 'enclosures' to be seen in an area of improved pasture. Bracken smothers the grass, and in autumn it is poisonous to cattle, so the farmer has eradicated it and re-sown the ground with better herbage. While this is undoubtedly better for the stock, the bright green looks out of place on these hills of naturally bleached grass, heather, and bracken which is a glory of red and gold in the autumn.

Go through the wicket gate and down left to another wicket gate which leads into the lower part of the plantation. Follow the path through the plantation.

Sitka spruce, which has a bluish tinge to its leaves, has been planted here. The leaves are hard and sharp and the blue-white stripes on them give the tree an overall blue appearance. This spruce was introduced from Canada in 1831.

Looking up the Breamish Valley towards Ritto Hill

Norway spruce, used for Christmas trees, is a native of nearly all European countries except Denmark and Holland. Excavations have shown that it grew in Britain in Upper Tertiary times, about 5 million years ago, before man was on earth. It has dull, dark green leaves which leave a tiny stump on the twig when they fall.

Lodgepole pine has needles of a brighter green, in pairs; they are broad and not densely set as in some pines, but spreading and twisted. This pine was introduced in 1854 from British Columbia and Alaska where it was used by Red Indians as poles for the framework of their lodges or wigwams.

Enter the field and walk across to a fence on the right which is followed to the gate at the confluence of the Shank Burn and the River Breamish. Retrace your outward route across the field below the cottage, turn right and follow the road to the starting point near Hartside.

West Hill seen from Bowl Holes

3 Ingram-Wether Hill-Cochrane Pike ; return via Old Fawdon Hill & Fawdon

About 8km, 3½ hours. This pleasant walk takes one up onto the hills without too much climbing and for most of the way the paths are quite distinct. There are good views on the return route.

Park at the car park by the toilet block and telephone kiosk just across the first bridge over the River Breamish at Ingram, approaching from the east (GR 018163). Walk along the road past the telephone kiosk to the corner, turn left and where the road bends to the left again, go through the field gate (R) signposted Prendwick. Walk up the slope beside the fence (L).

Grassy terraces can be seen on nearby hillsides, the work of medieval, or later, ploughmen. When the field is on a slope constant ploughing will cause some of the earth from the top of the field to slip down to the bottom and form a bank; this is known as a lynchet. In medieval times, a number of villagers farming in the 'open-field' system would have had such small cultivated 'fields' running across a hillside and separated by strips of unploughed land.

Cross the stile and turn right along the track which soon bears left and goes uphill through a gate.

You may be surprised to see an old kitchen sink sitting out on the hillside, or a small galvanised tub, or a dark coloured messy looking substance in a slit-open polythene bag. These strange containers hold a mineral 'lick' which supplies elements missing in the grazing ground. The sheep love them.

Walk straight on (over the stile by a gate) and follow the track which climbs gently for 800m. At the fork, go left and across an indistinct wet area, continuing downhill on a good path.

On a clear day the Simonside Hills south of Rothbury, come into view, and nearer to hand the hamlet of Prendwick lies half hidden in the

13

Orange tip butterfly

trees. Peaceful as it is today and seemingly far from Scotland, in the times of the Border Troubles from the late 13th - early 17th centuries, this area was ever on the alert. There were six men on watch from 'Prendeke to Engram' to give warning should the Scottish Reivers be seen riding over the hills to 'do a little lifting'.

About 120m before the gate leading to the enclosed field, turn left and walk down the sunken path, go through the gate and left uphill on a clear path. At the top of the steep bracken covered slope turn right. Follow the edge of the bracken down towards a fence seen ahead. About 100m before reaching it, turn left along an indistinct path with the fence to your right. The path gradually leads left away from the fence (R) and on towards the plantation and shed seen below Old Fawdon Hill (L).

There was another panic here in 1804 when Napoleon Bonaparte was thought to be invading England. The huge beacon on Ros Castle above Chillingham was fired and followed by those on hilltops in Alndale and Coquetdale. In the valleys of the Breamish, Aln and Coquet the Volunteer companies of the Cheviot region, the Coquetdale Rangers and the Percy Tenantry, were called out. There was great excitement and some fear. Tom Bolam 'had a pain in his breast' and felt far too ill to help but three glasses of whisky at 'The Fighting Cocks' put some spirit into him.

Willie Middlemas had a sudden pain and couldn't go out, Jack Dixon's horse needed

shoeing, so he couldn't ride. In fact it all turned out to be false alarm but as soon as it was known that the Volunteers would be given a good dinner at Collingwood House near Whittingham (about 3km to the south-east), everyone was overjoyed. Willie Middlemas's pain vanished; Jack Dixon found that his horse could trot quite well after all, and Tom Bolam was ready for anything. The dinner was a great success; some couldn't find their way home afterwards, and one Volunteer took his sword and beheaded all the cabbages in a nearby garden, just to show what he could have done to Boney's men.

Pass just to the right of the trees and the shed.

This has been a marshy area and only lately drained so the dampish soil is the place to find 'cuckoo flower', also called lady's smock. This flower appears with the cuckoo in early summer and may be white or lilac in colour. Some of the leaves form a rosette on the ground, but the ones on the stem are ladder-like. The orange tip butterfly lays its eggs on this plant. The female butterfly in search of the correct plant which will eventually feed her caterpillars, drums on the leaves with her front pair of feet. This releases some scent from the leaf surface, and in the butterfly the sense of taste is apparently conveyed from the feet to the brain, so the insect can judge whether or not the plant on which it has settled is the correct one to nurture its caterpillars. The butterfly flits from flower to flower, laying an egg here and there on the flower stalk or base of a bud. In this way the caterpillars are spread out, because they are cannabalistic and would eat each other if they were crowded together.

Walk down the track at the base of the steepest slopes of the hill, and continue, keeping left and above another plantation (R). Follow the fence (R) for 200m to a gate and a stile.

On a slope away to the right is a 'camp'; the ramparts and ditches are clearly seen. There are many of these scattered about the lower hillsides, some dating from the Bronze Age, around 2,500 years ago and some dating from the time the Romans were in Britain and

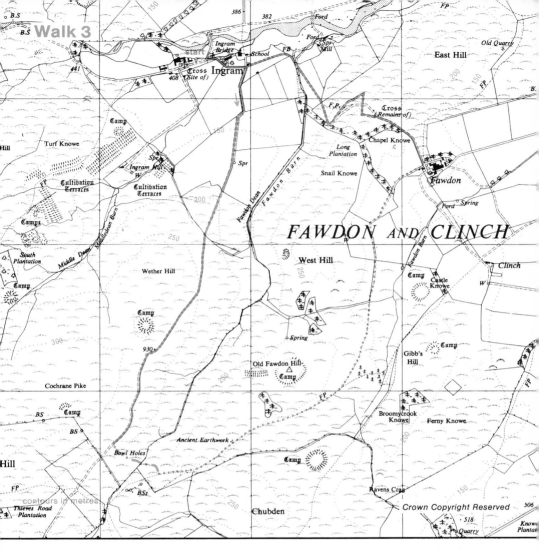

the presence of their soldiers made for a more settled way of life and less need for fortifications on hill tops. The economy of these settlements was essentially that of farmer and herdsman, and it was obviously a boon to be able to live down in the sheltered valleys and near a stream.

Cross the stile and walk down diagonally left across the field, through a gate and on towards a tall hedge, 100m uphill of the sheep pens (R). Two sets of gates are reached: go through the left-hand one and follow the path beside the hedge (R).

Everyone knows the old saying 'Cast not a clout till May be out' which refers to the blossom of the hawthorn or may tree. Hawthorns, also called 'quickthorns', make fine hedges when they are properly layered, forming a dense network with thorns which are a deterrent to man and beast; but birds find good nesting places amongst them, and, many enjoy the red fruits called 'haws'.

The hawthorn is the subject of many legends and much folk lore; many celebrations for the coming of summer are connected with the may tree, and it is said that Christ's crown of

15

thorns was made from hawthorn. When the blossom first appears it has an unpleasant smell of decay due to the presence of the chemical trinnethylamine; this attracts midges and flies which help to fertilise the tree. Later, the scent changes to a very pleasant one.

Blackthorn belongs to the *Prunus,* or plum family, and bears its starry white flowers in March and April; they show up well against the black bark. Blackthorns are more shrubby in appearance than hawthorns, and bear sloes as fruit. Their branches make good walking sticks.

The path leads below a line of trees (L) and on to pass a cottage at Fawdon. Go through the gate and turn left, uphill. Pass close to the trees at the top of the hill and follow the main track, which now zigzags down the hill, to a gate.

The Border Reivers passed this way. In 1587 some 500 men, mostly of the notorious Armstrong clan — or 'Riding Surname' — swept down from Scotland; they raided Ryle, Prendwick and Ingram, and drove 500 cattle, 300 sheep, and took 20 prisoners. Ingram

suffered a great deal from visitations of that sort.

Hedgehope Hill is seen ahead. Brough Law, crowned with the remains of an Iron Age hillfort, rises above the plantation to the left of the River Breamish.

Continue on the track through the field turning left to reach the road. At the road keep left and retrace your outward steps to the car park.

The church, just to the right, and opposite the National Park Information Centre, dates in part from the 11th-14th centuries. The tower was more than likely originally built for defence, being low and massive. It was taken down and rebuilt in the 19th century, all the old materials being re-used in their original positions.

The large house to the right, on the road back to the car park, is the old Rectory, now a private house as there is no longer a resident rector at Ingram. The size of the house shows that the village has shrunk from its original position of importance in the area.

Alwinton

This small village, the last in Coquetdale as you travel west, upriver, is beautifully situated at the foot of the Cheviot Hills. Sheltered from the north winds, looking across green haugh-land to the River Coquet and the heather clad fells beyond, it breathes an air of tranquility. It was not always so. From the 13th-17th centuries Alwinton suffered many raids from the Scottish Border Reivers, resulting in stolen cattle, burnt houses and men killed. Nearby Harbottle Castle was the military centre of the English Middle March, supported by ten towns — a 'town' was a cluster of farming communities — providing men and weapons. Alwinton was the first of the Ten Towns of Coquetdale, followed by Biddlestone, Clennell, Chirmundesden, Sharperton, Farnham, Burradon, Netherton, Fawdon and Ingram.

The church at Low Alwinton, just by the river bridge, is interesting and unusual; being built on a hillside there are ten steps from the nave to the chancel. A church warden's account of 1744 states that foxes (regarded as vermin) are to be paid for, providing the heads be fixed upon the church door.

Alwinton has a car park and toilets. Infrequent Post Buses run from Rothbury but times should be checked beforehand. Great care should be taken if driving up the valley beyond the village as the road is narrow and winding, sheep wander across it and farm or army vehicles from the military ranges may be encountered. The Otterburn Military Range, which borders the road on the left hand side above Alwinton is used as a live firing area. If the red flags are flying do not enter.

4 Alwinton-Clennell Street-Wholehope-Copper Snout ; return via Shillmoor & Pass Peth

13km, about 5 hours. This is a rather long and strenuous walk, following an ancient drove road for the first few miles. There is a stretch of rough hill walking, one or two short, but steep, climbs uphill and the last 1500 metres is along a metalled road. Choose a fine, clear day as there are good views towards the Border Hills.

Leave car at Alwinton car park (GR 919063), turn left at car park exit and walk a few metres along the road to a T-junction. Cross the village green and the footbridge, then turn left again to go up the track. Walk up the track keeping right past two farm entrances.

Clennell Street has been used for centuries. In Old English 'street' meant road, and this particular one must have been popular because in the main it follows the tops of the ridges avoiding the steep drops into, and climbs out of, the many valleys. Clennell Street runs for 19km from Alwinton to Cocklawfoot at the head of the River Bowmont in Scotland.

Border Reivers, smugglers, pedlars and drovers have all passed this way in their time.

The path winds on uphill through a gate, past a cottage (R), and after 1½km plantations on the right will be seen. Continue on the track.

On the left is Castle Hill with a prehistoric, probably Iron Age, hill-fort on its summit. There is another one on Clennell Hill, to the right above the valley of the River Alwin. On Lord's Seat the hill to the north of the Hosedon Burn gullies (L) are traces of cultivation of four different periods.

Go through gate bearing right on up the track past Uplaw Knowe (L). Pass sheep pens (L) and on skirting plantation go through a gate.

On the eastern side of Clennell Street, as it curves to the left around Uplaw Knowe, are traces of Romano-British settlements. These are not easy to see, but point to the fact that the area was inhabited long, long ago, and perhaps carried a greater population than it does now.

Walk up the slope to the ruin of Wholehope.

This was once a Youth Hostel but was found

West from sheepfold on Saughy Hill

to be too far off the beaten track to be properly managed, so was abandoned. Its walls make a good shelter for a lunch break.

The path leads just to the left of the ruin (through a gate), on by the wall to the forest and through another gate. Walk straight on up the track to a junction. Keep up left.

This is the western edge of Kidland Forest, owned by the Forestry Commission. The trees are Norway spruce. Spruces carry pendulous cones which fall bodily from the trees; in firs, the cones are erect and the cone scales are shed separately. The Norway spruce is grown for its timber, known as white deal.

It is easy to see that a woodland such as this does not offer much of a habitat for wildlife. The almost interlocking branches shut out the light and the fallen needles smother the ground.

At the end of the forest path, go through the gate, and walk on about 150m to a cairn. Now turn left across rough grassland and walk towards the corner of the plantation (L). Walk on with the fence to your left, and go through a gate (L) by a stell. Follow the faint track (it soon becomes much clearer) straight ahead, then bearing right over the low hill.

From here to Shillmoor this footpath crosses part of the dry training area of the Otterburn Military Range. Use of it is by courtesy of the Ministry of Defence and their tenant farmer. Do not be surprised if, in this area, you see troops training. There is no danger. Just keep to the footpath.

Wholehope Burn flows in the valley (L). To the right is the deep valley of the Usway Burn (pronounced Yoosy). In severe winters there have been snow slips on the steep slopes in this area, often causing the death of shepherds unfortunate enough to be caught in them.

Usway Burn rises on the flanks of The Cheviot and beside its upper reaches are the remains of Rory's Still — one of the many places in this remote area where illicit whisky was distilled. The liquor was carried to the isolated cottages in jars known as 'grey hens' and was called 'innocent whisky'.

The path now joins the stony track. Turn right and follow the track for 2km, over the hill almost to Shillmoor Farm.

The view to the right extends to the Border Hills. Another old drove road, called simply 'The Street', runs from the upper Coquet over the green hills and across the Border into Scotland. The long hill in the far distance is Beefstand, and to the right of it is Mozie Law.

19

The Pennine Way runs right along that ridge; it is one of the most exposed sections of the whole 434km walk from Edale in Derbyshire to Kirk Yetholm in Scotland.

Being so close to Scotland, this area was much devastated by the Scottish Reivers during the 300 years of Border turmoil that preceded the union of the Scottish and English crowns in 1603. The whole Border area from the Solway Firth to Berwick upon Tweed was divided on both sides into the West, Middle and East Marches. This area was in the English Middle March. Each March was in the charge of a Warden who found it no easy thing to control the clans, or 'Riding Surnames' as they were known. Due to inter-marriage and family feuds — and sometimes more than a dozen surnames were at feud at a given time — their loyalty was always questionable. Far from the seats of government in London and Edinburgh, the big surnames became a law unto themselves. Armstrongs, Halls, Forsters, Carletons, Elliots, Nobles, Storeys and a host of others liked nothing better than to ride by moonlight across the hills, rounding up and driving off such cattle as they could find, and if burning and bloodshed ensued, it was just hard luck. Scots against English, English against Scots — for 300 years it was a way of life. This area was almost uninhabitable until about the 18th century. A report in 1541 said it was impossible to encourage people to live here because of the frequent raids by the Scots, and the land being so divided and cut up by streams and hills the noise and commotion of a raid in one valley could not be heard in the next. By the time help was summoned, the cattle had gone.

Near the bottom of the hill follow the track round to the left with Shillmoor Farm below (R).

Wheatear

Walk 4

21

Shillmoor stands at the junction of the Usway Burn and the River Coquet. Before the bridge was built people had to cross the Coquet by a rocky, treacherous ford; many a horse-drawn conveyance has come to grief at Shillmoor ford. 'Stopped wi witters' is a phrase often found in official diaries.

Across the Coquet flies the red flag, a warning that the area is part of the Military Ranges and inaccessible to the public except at certain times, and then only the few roads will be open. Firing ceases for a few weeks each spring at lambing time; at other times shepherds go out over the hills when the guns are not in action. Farmers are compensated for stock losses caused by the military land-use. The Ministry of Defence owns about 20% of National Park land.

Keep on track past the Stell (L).

This is a fine example of a stell; it is in excellent condition. These dry-stone circular walls are built on sheltered parts of the hills where sheep can be gathered for attention during lambing or feeding in severe weather. Most Northumbrian stells are circular, but some may be square or even cross-shaped.

After Shillmoor reappears the track descends to meet a wall. Turn sharp left here to walk alongside the wall (R). Climb the stile to cross the Wholehope Burn. Follow the path

Dipper

straight on around The Knocks and above the River Coquet.

This is a pleasant spot for a rest. Wheatears, with their conspicuous white rumps, like this hillside, nesting in crevices among rocks or in old rabbit holes. Birds along the river include the grey wagtail, dipper and goosander, of which the latter — a saw-bill duck, is both the biggest and the least easy to see. It is a skilled fish-hunter and is controlled by trout farmers and bailiffs, hence it is a very shy bird and is most often seen flying up or down the river away from potential enemies.

The hillside has many wild flowers; heath bedstraw, a low-lying plant with white flowers, and tormentil, a little yellow flower. In olden days colic was cured by drinking milk in which the roots of tormentil had been boiled. In the Hebrides it was used as a tanning agent for fishing nets.

Germander speedwell is very common, its blue flower with a pronounced white eye — hence its name 'birdseye' — has inspired many poets to sing its praises.

Here, too, is bird's foot trefoil (sometimes called lady's slipper), a member of the pea family. The lowest pair of leaflets are bent back so that its leaves appear trefoil. The flowers are bright yellow, tinted with red, and the little seed pods, three or four in a cluster, resemble a bird's claw.

The path continues around the hill, crossing twin tracks to bear a little to the left to cross Passpeth Sike (a small stream). Two paths lead from this point. Ignore the lower indistinct one and go uphill from the sike to pick up a clear green path rising steeply up to the right to a dip at the hilltop (cairned).

The very steep slope above the Coquet had a snow slip in a severe winter some years ago which buried a flock of sheep sheltering at the bottom; a large number perished before they could be dug out.

The many little ridges running horizontally across the slope are the result of soil creep. Earth, loosened by the action of rain and frost, slips slowly downward and forms the little banks.

Copper Snout from Shillmoor track

Pass Peth is a historic path. In the days of the Border Troubles two men were on watch here, day and night, to give warning of any band of Scottish Reivers seen riding over the hills. A house at Linbriggs, the farm seen at the foot of the steep slope, was burnt and destroyed by the Scots in 1541.

About a hundred years ago there was a 'shepherds' school' at Linbriggs. The education of children living in the widely scattered cottages of this area was always a problem. The shepherds would club together and either engage a teacher at a fixed salary or offer him threepence a week for each scholar. He would live and board with a shepherd, as one of the family, for as many weeks as there were children in that cottage, and then move on to another family. The scholars would follow him, if the distance was not too far for them to walk.

Today the children travel quite a distance to school but by car or bus. The young ones go to Harbottle and the older children to Rothbury or Morpeth.

At the top of the slope walk straight on to cross a farm track and sike (in 500m), then up to the stile at the bottom edge of the cultivated field.

The steep cliffs of Barrow Scar (R) offer a fine exposure of cementstones laid down about 340 million years ago when most of Northumberland was covered by a shallow sea. Rivers from the Cheviots and the hills of southern Scotland carried sediments and deposited them in this sea which later receded and left the deposits to consolidate into rock.

Between the cliffs and the cottage of Barrow is Barrow Scrogs. 'Scar' means a rough, bare precipice and 'scrogs' is an area of brushwood.

Barrow House has, incorporated in its walls, stones of the old pele tower laid waste by the Scots in the early 16th century.

Go over the stile and follow the narrow path which follows the fence (L) and gradually descends the slope to a gate and stile in the fence 200m uphill of the cattle grid on the road. Cross the sike and bear right downhill on a well-worn path which leads in 300m to a wicket gate and road. Turn left and follow the road to Alwinton car park.

The sheep down here are Cheviots; they thrive better on the lower lands. One also gets a good view of the haughland — flat, grassy pasture by the river.

5 Alwinton-Clennell Street-Wholehope-Kidlandlee; return along the hillside west of the River Alwin

9km, about 3½ hours. This walk goes gently uphill along an ancient trackway, crosses a plantation where the path is a little overgrown and may be wet after rain, and returns above the River Alwin.

Leave car at Alwinton car park (GR 919063), and turn left at the car park exit to walk a few metres along the road to a T-junction. Cross the village green and the footbridge, then turn left again to go up the track, keeping right past two farm entrances.

The farmyard on the left shows how the farmers are moving with the times. The very large shed is used for over-wintering cattle; they thrive much better when properly fed and sheltered in a bad winter and one man can care for quite a number.

Some farmers also now bring their lambing flock down from the high hills in winter and pen them in large sheds like this one. The slatted sides give good ventilation, an important factor when animals are kept inside, as warm, stagnant air spreads disease. While the animals are inside the fields are rested and there will be clean pasture at lambing time. Farmers are obliged to consult with the National Park Authority over the siting and design of these sheds.

Beside the shed is a silo where grain or other feeding stuffs are stored for winter use.

Sometimes a silage pit is to be seen near a farmyard. Grass is cut in early summer and put in a pit. A large polythene sheet, often weighted down with old tyres, excludes the air and the mass ferments to become a most nutritious feed.

Walk up the track.

During the summer crosswort grows on the right side of the track, with tiny, pale yellow flowers geometrically positioned in whorls at the base of the leaves.

The path winds on uphill through a gate, past a cottage (R) and after 1½km plantations on the right will be seen. Continue on the track.

This track, called Clennell Street, runs for 19km over the hills to Cocklawfoot on the upper Bowmont River in Scotland. It is a very

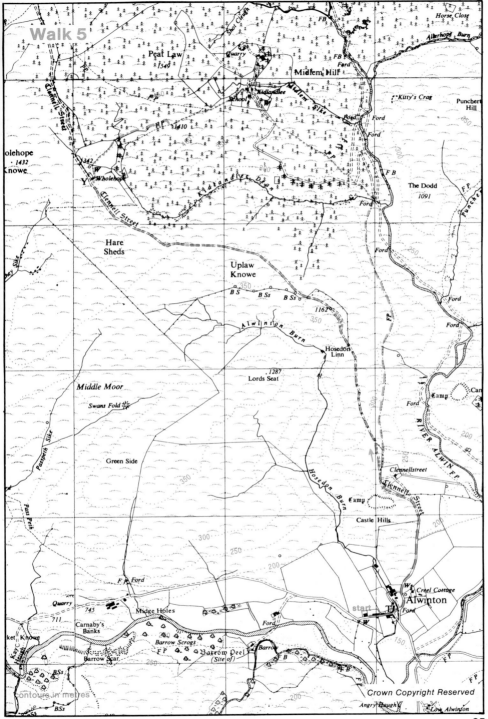

Walk 5

Peat Law
·1549

Shot Cleugh

FB

Horse Close

Aldhope Burn

Midlem Hill

Quarry

FB
Ford

Kitty's Crag

Puncher
Hill

Cloftield's Sted

Kidlandlee
School

Midlem Sike

Pond
Ford

Ford

olehope
·1432
Knowe

·342

Wholehope

Pond
F P

Ford

F B

The Dodd
1091

Puncher

Elsdonburn Dean

Kidlandlee Dean

Ford

F P

Hare
Sheds

Elsdon Street

Uplaw
Knowe

350

B S   B Ss   B Ss

1162°

350

Ford

Ford

Alwinton Burn

350

Hosedon
Linn

F P

Ford

Middle Moor

Swans Fold

·1287
Lords Seat

350

Green Side

Hosedon Burn

Camp

300

Clennellstreet

RIVER ALWIN F. P.

Clennell Street

200

350

Camp

Castle Hills

300

250

200

150

F P   Ford

Quarry
745

711

Midge Holes

Ford

Creel Cottage

Alwinton

start

Ford

Carnaby's
Banks

Barrow Scrogs

Barrow

W

F P

ket
Knowe

Barrow Scar

F P
(Site of)

Barrow Peel

B

250

B

150

F P

BSs

BSs

contours in metres

Crown Copyright Reserved

Angry Haugh

Low Alwinton

25

ancient route used by shepherds of long ago when taking their flocks to the shieling grounds or summer pasture; the herdsmen themselves lived in temporary shelters known as shielings. This practice continued well into the 18th century and only ceased with the enclosure movement. The word 'shiel' is still found in many Northumbrian place names, however.

Go through the gate bearing right on up the track past Uplaw Knowe (L). Pass sheep pens (L) and on skirting plantation, go through a gate and up to the ruin.

This is Wholehope, pronounced Woolup, all that remains of a one-time Youth Hostel. Too far from any supplies to be effectively managed, it survived for a few years as an

Ruin of Wholehope

experiment by the Mountain Bothy Association, left open on trust for all who needed its shelter.

'Hope' is another word often found in Northumberland place names. A 'hope' is an area of flat land and at the head of a valley, and thus of some value. In the past landowners sometimes bequeathed a 'hope' in their will.

Go through the gate immediately to the right of the ruin and cross the field to its top right hand corner. Leave the field via a wicket gate and walk on a few steps to a track. Turn right and follow the track for 50m until a grassy path leads left up the forest ride.

This is a damp spot hence the rushes and clumps of hair moss. Mosses have stems and leaves but no roots, only modified stems forming root-like structures. Male cells migrate through the water film on the plant surface to the female structure which has been found to secrete a chemical to guide them, so damp conditions are essential for reproduction. Once fertilised in this way the female receptacle develops a capsule which in turn produces spores, and these are dispersed by the wind to start new plants and colonies.

With the fence to your right walk to the fence corner. Turn right, and 20m later turn left. Follow the waymarking across the forest track, bearing left down a minor forest ride to walled enclosures at Kidlandlee.

This plantation of mainly Norway spruce, used as Christmas trees, was planted by the Forestry Commission.

The Forestry Commission was originally set up in 1919, after severe depredation of Britain's forests in World War I, to re-establish by new planting a future reserve of timber. It is now the largest grower in the country, helping to meet the timber industry's needs; much goes to United Kingdom pulp-mills and saw mills.

Many of the Commission's forests are open to the public to walk through, and there are often picnic sites and forest trails. Forest management is aimed at improving the appearance and wildlife habitat diversity of the forests — so making them more attractive.

Go through the gate and on down a narrow field between the walls towards a steel shed. Just before the shed turn right through a gate, then left through another gate to a gravel track.

Kidlandlee, standing at an altitude of 384m was built at the turn of the century as a shooting lodge. That sport having declined somewhat, the buildings have long been put to other purposes. The whole area of Kidland was a hunting ground in days long past. In 1181 the second Odinell de Umfraville leased the grazing to the Abbot of Newminster Abbey near Morpeth, but because it was a hunting ground, the monks were obliged to law their dogs, that is cut off 3 claws from the forepaw to prevent them chasing the Lord's game. Nearly 100 years later Culbert de Umfraville stated in a charter that he was unwilling for the souls of his father and ancestors to be in pain or peril by reason of the hunting rights he and his wife had retained over the gifts of the Cheviot Hills and Coquetdale moors to the monks of Newminster. Therefore he quit — claimed his rights and declared it was not lawful for any but the monks to hunt wolves and foxes on this land. De Umfraville is dead; Newminster Abbey was suppressed in 1536; the wolves have long gone, but the foxes are still here.

With your back to the cottages walk down the gravel track to a gate. Continue a short way on the track to leave it at the point where it turns right; go through the gate and along the grassy path beside the trees (L) to another gate and on down the forest ride.

Broom

Broom makes a splash of yellow beside the path in early summer. It has a distinctive way of distributing its pollen, releasing it into a pouch on one of the lower petals, which when a bee lands on it flicks upward thus spraying the insect with pollen. At the time of Henry II it was called *'planta o genista'* and was the badge of the King's father, the Count of Anjou. Henry adopted the plant and its name for his family, called in history books the Plantagenets.

Turn right, cross the cattle grid and go through the gate (R).

Some landowners use tubes or loose bars, which 'chatter' when a vehicle crosses them, to span the gap of a cattle grid, as they are a good deterrent to animals. Steel joists and old railway lines carry a heavier weight of traffic, however.

Care has to be taken over the side fencing, so that sheep cannot squeeze through a gap or even walk along the edge of the supporting walls of the pit. These walls have to be very carefully designed as they carry the load, not the bars. Some cattle grids now have little ramps in the pit to enable small animals, which have fallen in, to escape.

Walk uphill and after 50m fork left and follow the track as it winds above the valley.

The River Alwin (L) carries the water from many burns and sikes which drain the hills of Bloodybush Edge, Cushat Law and other lesser slopes, and joins the River Coquet just to the east of Alwinton. The road beside it runs up to the forestry plantations and has been surfaced with the red felsite from Harden Quarry at Biddlestone just over the hill to the left.

At the top of the climb the track turns sharply away right. Go straight on along a narrow sheep track, gradually bearing away from the valley (L). Contour around the hillside, across the top of a sike, then walk towards a gate when seen on the skyline. Cross the stile close by. Cross the field corner to another stile and then turn left down Clennell Street to Alwinton and your starting point.

There may be a herd of cattle in this field. They will be what is called a suckler herd. The calves suckle their dams until autumn when they are sold for fattening on lowland farms. They are cross-bred; those with big white faces have Hereford blood; the creamy-white ones, Charollais; the pale brown Simmental, and the short-haired black ones are likely to be a Limousin cross. The dumpy black long haired cattle are Aberdeen Angus. The farmer is endeavouring to produce an animal with firm, solidly-fleshed hind quarters, which is what the butchers look for in the sale ring at the fatstock market.

Occasionally one has to use a footpath crossing land where a bull is grazing with his herd. A beef bull is rarely temperamental but giving him a wide berth, walking quietly and close to a fence avoids trouble. Young stock, both bullocks and heifers, like all young creatures are often inquisitive and ready for a game. They may run after you but turning as if to chase them in return, soon sends them scattering. At certain times of the year the farmer may give them extra food; the animals seeing a walker crossing the field and perhaps carrying a bag are apt to rush up expectantly and look quite disappointed when nothing is forthcoming.

Where the forest ride bends left keep straight on down the narrow path. Cross a gravelled road, and on down in the same line left past a telegraph pole to the valley floor and another gravel road.

6 Clennell-Old Rookland-Puncherton; return via Loundon Hill & Rookland

Distance 9km, about 3½ hours. A walk along the quiet road beside the River Alwin, then a gentle uphill stretch beside a small burn and on to the hills. The middle section of this route follows no distinct path and the ground is rather rough, but later on it is a clear track. There are good views on the return walk.

Park on the grass by the roadside, a few metres before the start of the unmetalled road at Clennell (GR 928070). Cross the cattle grid by the footbridge and walk up the valley along the road crossing a bridge en-route.

The River Alwin — the name derives from the Old English meaning 'white' or clear water — drains the wet, peaty hills of Cushat Law and Bloodybush Edge. The whole area of Kidland, ahead, is shaped like the spread fingers of a hand; long steep ridges intersected by burns which all flow into the Alwin.

The trees on the hillside (R) have been so battered by winds whistling across and down this valley that they are all leaning over.

Cross the second bridge and cattle grid and turn immediately right, walking to the left of the Rookland Sike, which is the first one seen on the right-hand side of the valley since leaving Clennell.

River Alwin

In summertime pause a moment and listen for tic-tic-tic, the sound of the whinchat, a summer visitor to our land. This attractive bird has a brown speckled back, and the male has a pronounced broad white streak over its eye. It likes to perch on the top of bracken, and is usually heard before it is seen.

Walk beside the sike for about 1km.

Clumps of scaly male fern grow beside the burn; it likes acid soil and stony ground on hillsides, and is often found on screes. The stem is densely covered with bright orange scales, and when the leaves unfurl in spring they are yellowish green in colour.

Fern leaves are commonly known as fronds and when young are tightly coiled, unwinding as they expand. Spores are produced on the undersides of fronds in clusters of sacs called sori. They are formed from the parent plant without sexual fertilisation (like a cutting from a house plant), and when spores fall on to wet

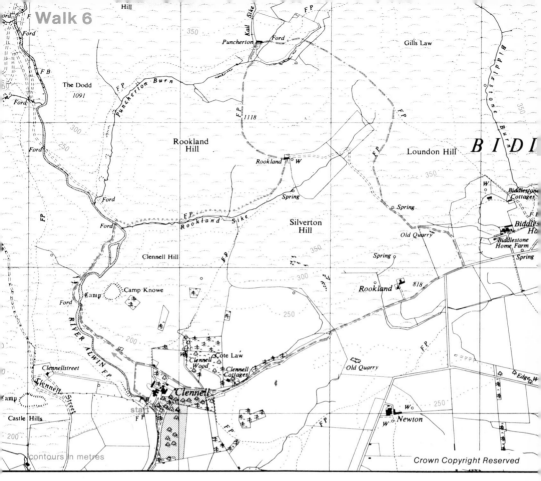

ground they develop into tiny heart-shaped structures which contain male and female reproductive parts. In wet conditions the male cells migrate through the water on the plant's surface to the female receptacle, and the new fern grows directly from that.

Go through the gate and gradually bear left uphill, away from the sike (cairned). Continue for 300m up to the ruins.

Few shepherds today would wish to live in such a house, with no services and no road to it. However the walls give shelter for sheep, which can be fed here in bad winters.

At Old Rookland go through the gate on the left and up to corner of the ruin. Turn left and follow the track towards a gate then bear right to a stile in the fence (70m from the gate). Cross the stile and bear right across rough ground (cairned). When Puncherton Farm is seen below, walk down towards it and cross the burn to a gate between the two sikes seen running on either side of the farm.

The stream is Puncherton Burn flowing west-wards to add more water to the River Alwin.

Walk through the gate and up the slope with the wall to your right (please keep dogs on a lead).

Puncherton is certainly 'far from the madding crowd'. Land here was once given as a gift to Brinkburn Priory.

31

Turn right at the gate and walk through the farmyard and continue up the farm track.

On hill farms the land is divided into inbye and outbye. Inbye lies close to the farmstead, like the fields here, near the house. The farmer uses inbye fields as good grazing for his house cows, riding horses and sheep at lambing time. He is likely to have a hayfield here and perhaps some rootcrops to fatten lambs. Outbye is the rough hill grazing where the sheep, Scotch blackface or Swaledales, forage for most of the year. Always take great care when crossing inbye land, so as not to interfere with the farmer's arrangements.

Leave the field by a gate, and after a ford is crossed follow the track uphill, which after a while passes through another gate.

Down below, to the right, is the ruin of Old Rookland, passed on the way to Puncherton. Ahead, the view opens up across Coquetdale to the Simonside Hills. Some 300 million years ago a shallow sea covered the low-lying area before you, and deposited beds of mud and limestone. Much later the sea re-treated and the soft rocks then exposed were eroded by ice during the Ice Age. When this

ice finally melted it left more deposits which were weathered into fertile soil. The many small woods seen scattered about were planted as shelter belts for stock, crops and dwellings.

Follow the track, curving right, to another gate after 400m. Continue on the clearest track downhill for 500m to a track fork. Go left and through a gate to cross a field to a road.

The small quarry on the right is one of many to be found on these hills. The landowner will have built dykes and stells from stone taken from his hillsides. Most of the dry-stone walls, or dykes as they are called in Northumberland, date from the 18th and 19th centuries. The average life of a well-built dry-stone dyke is about 200 years.

Away to the left is a different type of quarry, very busy at the moment. It is the Harden Quarry at Biddlestone, extracting red felsite which is used for road surfacing.

At the road turn right, follow it for a short distance and at the point where it turns left walk straight on through the gate and past Rookland House (R).

Near the gate, opposite Rookland House, is a patch of yellow rattle, also called cock's comb. It is an erect, stiff plant; the yellow flowers are two-lipped, usually open-mouthed and often with two purple teeth, blooming all summer on leafy spikes. When the fruit cap-sules are dry, the seeds rattle inside. This plant is interesting because it is partially parasitic, securing some nourishment from the roots of grasses.

Follow the track gently downhill through several fields and gates, passing a plantation (R) to a gate. Through the gate, pass Clennell cottages (R) and after 100m the track bears right to another gate. Go through this and on down the tree-lined avenue to a house (R). Pass in front of the house and through the gate immediately on the right.

Clennell Hall is to your left. This house began as a 14th century pele tower, still to be seen at the right of the house, incorporated in the newer building. Clennell was first mentioned

Harden Quarry

in 1181 and there were Clennells here in 1228 when the Abbot and monks of Newminster Abbey entered into agreement with Thomas of Clennell about wayleave for their cattle to go up the Alwin Valley to their shiels, or summer grazing, at Kidland. In return for this favour the monks promised Thomas that he should be remembered in their prayers and every year at Martinmas he should receive a pair of boots.

In 1895 the Hall was extended, and the village was cleared away to make room for gardens and a park.

The name Clennell means 'clean hills', or one free from trees.

Turn left to follow the wall (L) to a gate by the red gravel road. Turn left down the road to return to your starting point.

7 Biddlestone Townfoot-Singmoor Cottage; return via Singmoor & Harden Hill

5½km, about 2½ hours. A short and easy uphill walk to the moor, then an almost level stretch across the grass and heather in a peaceful, 'off-the-beaten-track' area.

Park carefully at the T-junction at Biddlestone (GR 961083). Walk uphill on the road for 30m towards a quarry and turn right along the road signposted 'Biddlestone Town Foot'. Go through the first gate on your left (300m along the road) and straight up across the field to a wicket gate at the highest point of the field. Go immediately left through a gate and onto a track.

The red felsite that is being dug out of Harden Quarry was formed some 300 million years ago when a dome shaped mass of molten material welled up from within the earth, to form what is called a laccolith. It pushed the overlying rocks upwards in a buckled arch, and gradually cooled beneath them into a hard, red rock. Harden felsite has been used to surface many roads; it was taken to London to make a road of 'red carpet' along the Mall to Buckingham Palace.

Turn right, follow the track uphill keeping right at a fork. Go up through the gate and walk along the track which winds, then curves left and in 400m passes a stell (R).

Stells are stone walled enclosures used for sheltering sheep.

Follow the track down the dip and up through the gate and on through another gate just past the cottage of Singmoor.

Shepherds today find it too inconvenient to live in these isolated cottages with no facilities and far from schools.

The shepherd likes to inspect his flock twice daily, morning and late afternoon. He will cover his territory on horseback, in a Land-rover, or maybe a scrambler bike.

Simonside Hills from lower slopes of Bleakmoor

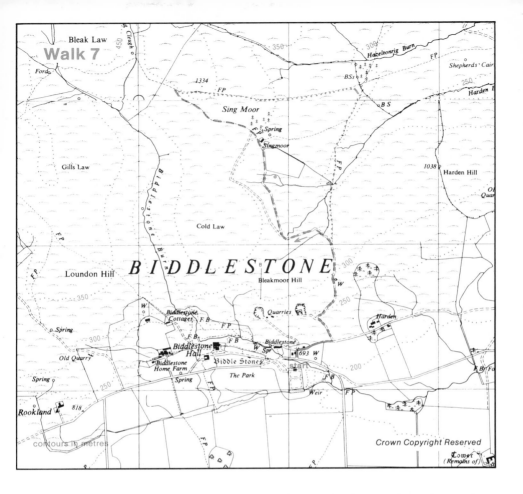

The flock on a hill farm is usually 'tied'; a farmer selling the farm sells the stock with it, because they are acclimatized to the land. A 'hirsel' is an area of hill with natural boundaries which is normally shepherded by one man. A hirsel may contain several 'hefts', or groups of sheep which habitually graze within the confines of a particular hill area. Each year some ewe lambs are kept to replenish the flocks on the hefts. Hill sheep do not wander all over the hills; they are born and bred to their heft and stay within its confines. They know where the best 'spring bite' is to be found, where to find water and shelter from the weather.

The sheep-dogs, usually black and white Border Collies, are bred for speed, intelligence and obedience. Northumbrian sheep dogs are famous for these traits and many have been exported abroad.

Walk up to the left of the plantation to its corner, then follow the rather indistinct path uphill as it turns slightly left, and then continue for about 400m.

The long bubbling call of the curlew (emblem of Northumberland National Park) is often heard on moors like this, where it breeds. It is Europe's largest wader and is easily recognisable, having a very long, down-curved bill with which it extracts worms and insects from boggy ground.

The path now bends slightly right. Walk on a few metres to pass a track coming in

from the left. Continue up the track for 200m and at a cairn 100m before gate, turn sharp right across the moor (cairned) and descend past the top of Singmoor Plantation (R). Continue descending slightly left with Hazeltonrig Burn down in the dip to the left.

Heather flourishes where the presence of impermeable granite creates an acid, peaty soil. Ling *(Calluna vulgaris)* carries pale purple flowers in leafy stalked spikes towards the end of summer. Bell heather *(Erica cinerea)* flowers earlier, its deeper coloured, red-purple flowers blooming from May to September. In wetter patches of moor cross-leaved heath *(Erica tetralix)* may be found, although never in extensive tracts like ling. It is an attractive plant, with its cluster of pink flowers in a compact head at the tip of the stem.

Walk on about 400m to reach a gate at the right-hand corner of a plantation. Without going through the gate turn sharply right to walk along a path for 500m.

On a warm summer's day skylarks may be singing overhead. These birds have white outer feathers on the tail and a short rounded crest on the head. They do not hop, but walk, and never perch on branches. Another, rather similar bird frequently seen on these grassy hills is the meadow pipit. It is a little smaller than the skylark and has no crest, but it does have the white outer tail feathers. Both these species nest in rough grass, so the lower slopes of the Cheviots make a good habitat for them.

Walk towards the sheep pens and go through the gate (L) beside them. Follow the track into a dip and up to the right-hand gate. Follow the track by a fence (L) and after 300m bear slightly right to rejoin the Singmoor track. Retrace the outward route back to the starting point.

Biddlestone Hall, now demolished, stood among the trees to the right of the quarry. Edward I granted the lands to Walter de Selby, whose brave and warlike family was frequently involved in the Border raids; few heads of the house died in their beds. Biddlestone is said to be the original of Osbaldistone Hall in Sir Walter Scott's Rob Roy.

Alnham

Yeldom is the local name for this hamlet, and there have been many other variations through the ages — Yarwell, Elnham, Alenam, to mention only a few.

A cluster of cottages, farms and a church, Alnham lies near the source of the River Aln which flows on past Whittingham and Alnwick to the sea at Alnmouth.

It was once a place of some importance. On the hill opposite the church stood a tower, first mentioned in 1405, but burnt in a raid by the Scots in 1532. In the last century many stones from the fallen castle walls were used to build walls around the fields on the adjoining farms.

Beside the church is the old vicarage, now privately owned. At the eastern end of this building is a restored 'vicar's pele' or fortified house. This pele was mentioned in 1541. During the 300 years of Border Troubles, from Edward I's annexation of Scotland in the 13th century until the Union of the Crowns in the 17th century, safety in the Border region depended upon a weapon to hand, the support of the clan or Riding Surname, the power of the Warden of the March, and a fortified dwellinghouse. Livestock was put in the base of the tower for safety, and the family lived upstairs. The stairs themselves were usually of stone to prevent fire, but even so the Reivers had a nasty habit of breaking down the door and lighting a bonfire at the entrance to smoke out the inhabitants. Of course the same type of building was in occupation on the Scottish Borderlands against the ravages of the English Reivers. It was a two-way traffic.

This pele is said to be haunted.

There is no bus service to Alnham but Post Buses may run at certain times.

Alnham Church

8 Alnham-Northfieldhead Hill-White Gate; return via Hazeltonrig

8km, about 3½ hours. A pleasant, not too strenuous walk with a short, easy uphill stretch followed by gently undulating ground. Hazeltonrig is an attractive, wooded spot. For most of the way there is a clear path.

Park on the grass by the Alnham Church of St Michael and All Angels (GR 991109).

Tradition says that this church is built on the site of a Roman camp. It was probably first built by the lord of the manor, but in the 12th century it belonged to the monks of Alnwick Abbey. In the 19th century the building was in a deplorable condition but repairs were put in hand and the church is still in use. The Parish extends for nearly 5,000 hectares, right over the hills, nearly to the summit of The Cheviot itself, but there are less than 100 souls within it. Near the lych gate are three ancient socketed bases for crosses.

Walk alongside the road a few steps, past the vicarage and its pele tower, then turn right up a track beside the vicarage garden wall. Go through the gate and walk uphill beside the wall (L). Pass the plantation (R) to a gate. Go through the gate and up by a wood (L) and then by a wall to a gate. Go through this gate and right over a little burn, walking beside it, bearing right away from the wall. A ruin and track is reached in 200m. Turn left up the track to the top of a rise. As the track bends right (20m before fence) leave the track, walk straight on and cross a stile. Follow a sunken grassy track to cross the Coppath Burn in 400m. Now bear left to the wall.

These hills are called the White Lands because the predominant vegetation, matgrass, bleaches almost white at the end of summer. Sheep find this grass rough and unpalatable. Even though the grazing is not the richest these rolling uplands of windswept, cloud-dappled, sun-bleached grass are the very essence of the Cheviot Hills, and the National Park Authority wishes to maintain their character.

Watch carefully for a gate in the wall (L). Walk towards it.

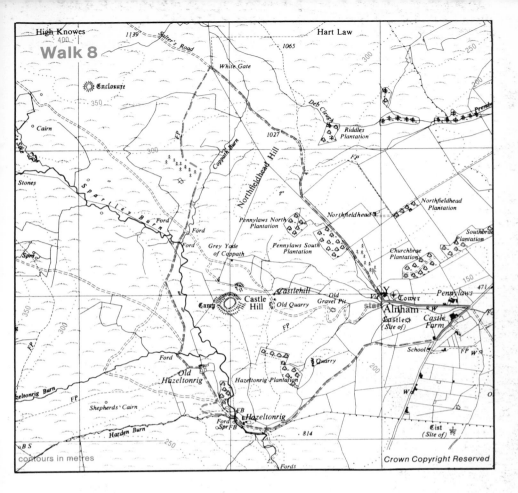

This path is the Salter's Road along which salt was carried from the salt pans on the coast to Scotland. Those who have walked from Alnham Moor to Low Bleakhope will have seen this track from Little Dod. It is the path trodden by the wedding party whose happy roisterings were described in that walk.

Go through the gate.

This is White Gate. A 'gate' or 'yett' was an opening or entrance to an area, not necessarily a man-made barrier. It also meant a stint, or right of pasture. 1 stint = 1 cattle gate. 5 sheep = 1 stint. A cowgate is a stint. The word 'white' may have referred to the bleached grasses.

With your back to the gate bear to the left

and walk across rough grassland for 400m. When the plantation ahead is seen, walk towards its left lower corner.

Kestrels like to hunt over this type of country. The bird is often called the windhover from its habit of apparently hanging motionless in the air, hovering head to wind, supported by a rapid vibration of its wings. Kestrels are helpful to farmers because they rid the ground of many pests. Possessing outstandingly keen vision, a kestrel can sight a field mouse from a height of 15m.

Walk between the plantation (R) and the Coppath Burn. Follow grassy track above burn (stells in view on right) to road.

◀ *Pennywell House, Alnham*

These circular stone walls were much used in the past for sheltering sheep, especially at lambing time. A few hurdles or straw bales would divide the stell into temporary 'rooms' where ailing sheep or weak lambs could be kept under observation.

Cross the road just to the right of the small bridge.

The red and white pole is a snow marker to indicate the road when the whole area is feet deep in snow. In olden days when shepherds and their families walked miles across the hills from the market, or friends' houses, there were many tragedies in winter-time when sudden heavy snowfalls or 'whiteouts' obscured all landmarks. The road is a continuation of the one the walk started upon and leads to the farm of Shank House about 1 1/2km further on.

Walk a few metres parallel to the burn (L). Cross the small Spartley Burn and then bear right to walk up the slope to the gate.

There are the remains of Romano-British settlements in this area, but they are hard to see on the ground among the grass and bracken.

Go through the gate and follow the path to the left on the hillside above the burn.

To the left is Castle Hill, on the summit of which are the remains of an Iron Age hillfort constructed and lived in some 2,500 years ago. Part of the ramparts can be seen on the skyline. There is much evidence of prehistoric life in this area in hillforts, settlements and burial grounds.

Follow the track as it leads down to the Hazeltonrig Burn, crossing it to the right of the farm buildings seen ahead.

Walk seven described in this book going from Biddlestone Town Foot to Singmoor met this burn a little way to the right, upstream.

Walk up the slope and through a gate and left on the track to some barns.

There is a Dyers' Field nearby, so Hazeltonrig is probably the site of the fulling mill known to exist near Alnham in the 18th century, and perhaps earlier. The dyeing, carding, spinning and weaving of wool were cottage industries carried out in the shepherds' homes. A fuller catered for all the weavers in a given area. The cloth was immersed in water and with the user of Fullers' Earth, a type of clay, it was 'walked' to remove the natural grease and to felt the fabric. Later, this 'walking' was reproduced by a set of wooden mallets activated by tappets and turned by a water wheel. After fulling the cloth was stretched on tenter frames and dried in the sun and wind: hence the phrase 'to be on tenter hooks'.

Follow the track right, through two gates and go down to cross the burn by the bridge.

The suffix of Hazeltonrig is probably derived from the word rig, or rigg, meaning ridge. In medieval times the arable land was divided into strips separated by grassy banks or paths. A villager's strips were not side by side but scattered about the whole area of cultivated land. There was a periodic exchange of strips for a more even distribution of good and not so good land. This system of re-allocation was known as 'run-rig'.

Continue on the track and pass in front of Hazeltonrig bungalow, then take the path to the left uphill, before the next gate.

When the gorse is in full flower in early summer, the whole hillside is perfumed by its coconut smell. The leaves of the gorse are modified thorns, and this protects it from the worst ravages of browsing animals. Gorse transpires so much water that it can dry out areas of damp ground. On dry, warm summer days the bush crackles. This noise is caused by sudden expulsions of seeds from the dry pods, which are thrown some distance away, thus extending the plant's territory. Whin, and furze, are other names for this bush, the bark of which was once used in Scotland to produce a yellow dye.

Hazeltonrig

Go through the gate and follow the track by a fence (L) to a gate. Go through the gate and follow the track across the field to another gate. Walk on 100m to a fourth gate by the wall end.

This now peaceful area suffered much from the Border warfare. In 1532 the Earl of Northumberland wrote to Henry VIII complaining that the 'Scottes of Tyndale with the nombre of 300 personages and above… brunte a town of myne called Alenam, with allits corne, hay, household stuf, also a woman'. However, it was not all one-sided, as the Earl on another occasion told the King he would 'lett secretle slippe' men for the annoyance of Scotland and 'may God send them all good spede'.

Go through the gate and along a track bearing right through another gate, which leads to the road just to the right of the red roofed buildings. At the road turn left, and then after 400m left again for Alnham Church.

Hepple

This attractive small village, some 8km west of Rothbury on the B6341, lies in lovely countryside. There are fine sweeps of high undulating moorland covered with heather and bracken and studded with ancient earthworks.

As long ago as 1265 Hepple was an important lordship held direct from the king possessing capital rights, a gallows, an assize of ale and bread and other privileges of the time not held by any other manor in the area except Rothbury.

The area was much harassed by raiding Scots during the 300 years of Border Troubles from the late 13th - early 17th centuries. There were several pele towers, or fortified houses nearby, and the following walk passes quite close to the ruins of Hepple Tower, the walls of which were found to be so strong that an attempt to use the stone to build a farmstead was abandoned.

There is a bus service to Hepple from Rothbury, but times should be checked beforehand.

Hepple village

Hepple church from West Hepple road end

9 Hepple bridge-West Hepple-Holystone-Lady's Well-Wood Hall; return via Sharperton-High and Low Farnham & Wreighill

11km, about 4½ hours. This walk may be taken as a whole, or shortened by leaving out the Holystone, Lady's Well, Wood Hall section which makes a very pleasant, easy stroll on its own of just 4km, about 1½ hours. Directions are given in the text.

The Holystone section is on level ground but High and Low Farnham are on a hillside and there are good views along that route. The walk is across agricultural land and crops change from year to year. Sometimes there is grass, sometimes one has to walk beside a cornfield where the edges may be a bit overgrown.

Park in the layby on the north (Hepple Village) side of the bridge (GR 982003). Walk uphill towards Hepple and take the first turning left (after 400m) signposted West Hepple.

The Grasslees Burn (L) flows through a pretty wooded valley. There are ramparts and ditches of Iron Age encampments on the hills, and on the lower ground several sites or remains of pele towers built in the 14th and 15th centuries as a refuge from marauding Scots. The hills away to the left are part of the Ministry of Defence military ranges and are inaccessible to the public.

The road leads past houses (R) and up to West Hepple Farm.

The house was built partly from the ruins of an old chapel nearby, the walls of which were cleared away in the 18th and 19th centuries to facilitate farming.

Pass to the right side of the house and farm buildings and walk out of the farmyard on the right. After 20m turn left along the track. At the end of the farm sheds turn right through a gate and up a track (hedge on right). This soon bears left to a gate.

This is Kirk Hill, the site of the old chapel ruined by Scottish raiders. A cross was erected to mark the spot, and the Norman font bowl is now in Hepple church. The remains of the chapel were removed about 1760.

Go through the gate and turn right.

The River Coquet flows below (L). The gravel reaches show that this river is liable to flood and make new channels for itself. Wading birds such as the oyster catcher, a large black and white bird with a red bill, and the common sandpiper favour these quiet reaches.

Notice three long plantations ahead; the path runs just below them. Follow the way-marking arrows on the gate posts indicating the route across the fields. The route is all downhill to a gate, after which the track rises. Turn left here and with a fence on your left walk 100m to a plantation. Turn right and walk beside it (trees on left), crossing a stile en-route.

All these plantations are shelter belts, with the timber being sold after about 40 years to be used for chipboard or in paper-making. Across the river are large Forestry Commission plantations covering a much wider area. Most of the trees here are Norway spruce, the Christmas tree.

Cross the small bridge (L) at the end of plantation and turn right to walk on below these long plantations.

Silverweed grows in the damp places by the burn (R). The undersides of the leaves are covered with a silky down which gives them an attractive silvery appearance. The yellow flowers bloom throughout the summer. This plant can become a nuisance, as it produces numerous runners which cover the ground with new growth.

In these plantations notice the Sitka spruce (it has a bluish look due to the blue-white bands beneath the leaves) and larch, usually Japanese larch, one of the few deciduous conifers. Larch can grow to a height of 30m, but its cones are quite small and egg shaped.

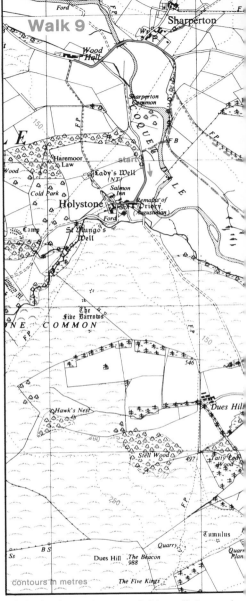

With the fence to your right, walk towards the long white-painted footbridge, 1km away. (Note: If drainage ditches are flooded make a detour out into the field and then rejoin the fence).

The cluster of cottages across the river is Holystone. The bridge is of unusual length

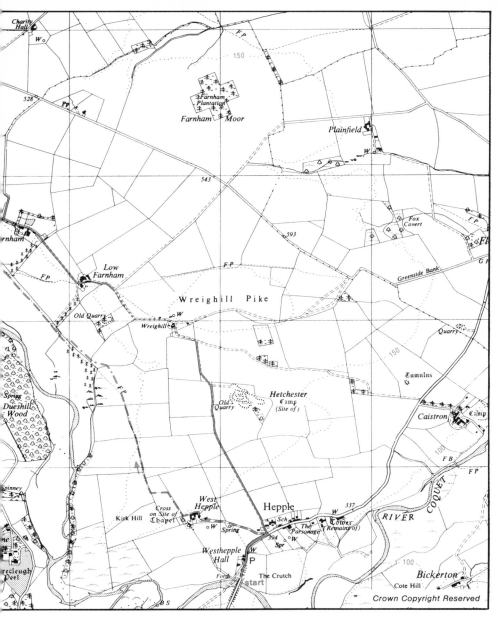

Crown Copyright Reserved

because when the Coquet is in flood, this low lying land known as haughland is under water.

Cross the footbridge and walk ahead on a track to the road. Turn left.

(The Holystone/Lady's Well walk starts here. **Park at the roadside near the footbridge over the River Coquet just west of Holystone on the Harbottle/Holystone road — (GR 956031), taking care not to obstruct gateways).**

Walk towards Holystone Village on the road.

Lady's Well

Holystone, tucked away between wooded hills and the River Coquet, was once quite a sizeable place, having a corn mill, a blacksmith's forge, and a weaver and dyer. Tailors, shoe-makers, masons, joiners and besom makers made up the workforce which supplied the community with its needs. The village gradually declined, however, and the extinction of the common rights in the last century accelerated the process.

It is not known how the village got its name but tradition says that there was a holy stone near the Coquet where a missionary preached the Gospel. A priory of Augustinian nuns was founded here in the 12th century. The Prioress, because the nuns held land in Roxburgh, was among the nobles and clergy who did homage to Edward I at Berwick in 1296. This attempt of Edward to make himself King of all Britain resulted in 300 years of Border Troubles. Holystone suffered severely from Scottish raids and by 1312 the Priory was reduced to poverty. Almost defenceless against attack, the nuns fled to Newcastle for a period in 1322. The Priory was dissolved in 1539 and the remaining seven nuns pensioned-off. The buildings, situated south of the present church, were demolished and the stones used in reconstruction work at Harbottle Castle.

Turn right at the road junction and walk through the village until just before the Salmon Inn car park. Follow the signposted path to the Lady's Well, hidden in the trees (L).

The derivation of the name is uncertain; perhaps it was connected with the nuns. The conversion of the well into a rectangular basin with stone walls may date from pre-Reformation times. By the 18th century the walls were in ruins, but the basin was repaired in 1780 and the statue brought from Alnwick

Castle. The story that Paulinus baptized thousands of Northumbrians in this pool is considered doubtful. A notice board just inside the gate gives the history of the well.

A Roman road passed by the site of the Lady's Well on its way from Rochester *(Bremenium)* near Otterburn to join the Devil's Causeway near Bridge of Aln, south of Powburn.

The path goes straight on through the right-hand gate and across the field on a track to a narrow belt of trees by a barn.

A shelter belt of deciduous trees was planted on the slopes of the hill (L) during the 18th century in a not too successful effort to improve the moorland. The wood is now swamped by the dark conifers of Forestry Commission plantations.

On these fields you may find lapwing or peewits, also called green plover. They are the farmer's friend, feeding on grubs and other insects. Seen from a distance the lapwing appears a black and white bird, but the upper parts have a beautiful metallic green lustre. During the mating season lapwings make tumbling 'display' flights; this, and the plaintive 'peewit' cry are the very essence of hill country.

Go through the gate and straight on to a stile after 50m. Now follow a fence (L) across the field to the left end of a small belt of pine trees. Cross the stile and go straight on up a grass track (fence on right) for 200m to a gate (R). Go through the gate and along the track to a road.

Wood Hall is ahead. 'Hall' seems a grandiose name for what is often seen to be a small farmhouse and its attendance row of cottages. In early times when cottages were mere hovels thatched with turf or heather, the Hall would have been a better, stone built house but not necessarily a mansion.

Turn right at the road and walk to the T-junction. (Those on the Holystone/Lady's Well walk can either go down the road on the right to the car park a couple of hundred metres away, or walk on a little further).

Continue across the bridge.

The bridge at Sharperton was opened in 1879 and re-constructed in 1920. Before that travellers had to use a wide and rather tricky ford away to the left. In days gone by these fords across the Coquet, treacherous in times of flood, took a heavy toll of life. The Coquet, narrow and shallow as it appears, has never been a river to trifle with.

Walk on road past the hamlet on left.

Sharperton is just a tiny place, but it was mentioned far back in history. In 1244 a certain Thomas of Sharperton was amongst the jurors at the inquest into the death of the great Lord Gilbert I de Umfraville of Harbottle Castle, who had almost regal powers in this part of the world. He held the Barony of Prudhoe as well as the Lordship of Redesdale.

Oystercatchers

A good friend to the English king, Gilbert was once described as 'the Guardian and Chief Flower of the North'. Also with his place in history, but for a lesser reason, is Richard Horseley, who in 1311 complained loudly of a raid upon his sheep at Alwinton made by the men of Sharperton, including the chaplain. Reiving in those days was a way of life and carried no disgrace, and the loser would wait his chance to go a-reiving in turn.

Village squabbles went on then as now. In 1682 George Potts of Holystone made a will leaving 'to my sister Ann Potts of Sharperton, a cow's grass and a house to sitt in so long as she lives', but some time later they fell out and in 1687 Ann complained that 'George Potts of Holystone came with force and arms as she was gathering small shrubs and graines for firewood in ye wellfield and then and there threatened to kill her with his sword and brought a large roap and threatened to hang her'. History gives no more of this sibling squabble.

Another Potts, Michael by name and a vintner, went from Sharperton to bear witness against Charles I at his trial in 1648-9.

Walk along the road a short distance to a sharp left bend. At this point go through a gate in the fence (R) down across a ditch and up the bank through the trees (fence to your left), to a wicket gate. (At this point above the trees, the Holystone/Lady's Well walkers follow the fence (R) to go down to the large footbridge which is crossed to reach the starting point).

Those going to Hepple walk straight on up across the hillside, past the two large stone gateposts and along the line of felled trees.

A glance back shows the Coquet flowing through haughland, with the ruins of Harbottle Castle in the trees to the left of the river. Beyond that lies Alwinton backed by the Cheviot Hills.

Cross the stile and walk to the lower right-hand corner of the plantation seen ahead. Walk alongside the plantation (L) to continue beside a similar plantation (L), and through a gate at the road. Turn right.

High Farnham is on the left. There was a pele tower here in 1415, but in 1546 it was burnt by 50 men of the Teviotdale and the only trace of it today is a circular stone-lined well among the trees on the north side of the present farmhouse. In its time it was of some importance, garrisoning 20 men in 1509 and they were needed: 50 men of Teviotdale, in 1546, rode up and burnt 'Thanham', as it was then called, in order to draw the Countrymen into an ambush.

Walk along the road through High Farnham to Low Farnham.

Green woodpeckers live among these trees. The bird's loud, laughing call has given it the name 'yaffle'. Woodpeckers like old trees because of the insects they harbour. To support itself while working on a vertical tree trunk, the bird has developed sharp claws on two toes facing forward and two backwards. The very stiff feathers of the pointed tail also help it to hold its position. The woodpecker's long thread-like tongue seeks out insects lurking beneath the bark.

The road passes through the buildings of Low Farnham.

In the 19th century many flint implements were found in fields hereabouts. There is no flint in this area; it occurs naturally in chalk and was formed from sponges and so was presumably brought here and traded for other goods in Neolithic or Bronze Age times.

Farming here is concerned with the raising of beef cattle, some sheep and arable crops, usually barley. This is recognisable by its long whiskers or awns. The best barley goes for brewing, but most is used for animal feeding. A field of intense yellow in early summer contains oilseed rape, grown for its oil. Bee keepers don't like it because it causes the honey to deteriorate quickly.

Follow the road and after 200m leave it at a sharp left bend and proceed over a cattle grid and up the track. Follow the track to Wreighill.

The local pronunciation is Wreehill. There isn't much to see now, but it has had its day. The name is said to be derived from Wearghill, the 'felons' or 'gallows hill'. In olden days a beacon was always in readiness on the hill behind the cottages, but the lighting of it did not always bring sufficient aid, for in 1412 the hamlet was wiped out in a Scottish raid.

It re-established itself, but a disaster struck again in 1665 when a Miss Handyside received a parcel from London. Soon afterwards she fell ill and died of the plague and almost

51

everyone else in the place followed her to the grave. As plague is carried by fleas it is possible that some hopped out of the parcel. The dead were buried in such places as it was supposed neither spade nor plough would turn up, but in the last century men quarrying the limestone for a nearby kiln came upon a large quantity of human bones, thought to be those of the victims.

Wreighill made another attempt to get on its feet, and produced in 1752 George Coughron whose intelligence was such that he became a mathematical prodigy and took up work as calculator to the Astronomer Royal. He died when only twenty years old.

In 1816 twenty people were living at Wreighill, but it has sunk into obscurity again.

Walk to the right by the first barn (R), not up to the cottage on the slope. Go over the cattle grid and up to the gate where the right fork in the track is taken. Follow the track down a dip and up the far slope (past quarries on right and left). Then downhill again to a track fork just before a gate.

To the left is Hetchester Camp, a prehistoric settlement much damaged by quarrying. Many interesting objects have been found there, querns used for grinding corn, Roman coins and red deer antlers.

Hepple Tower

Ahead there are glimpses of lakes. This is the Caistron Gravel Works. The firm, Ryton Gravel Co Ltd, have made the disused pits into a fascinating nature reserve; the water-filled pits and specially planted trees and vegetation encourage wildlife, and hides have been placed for bird watchers. The Reserve Warden conducts the public around the area at certain times.

It was on a farm near Caistron that at the turn of the 19th century the iron plough was first introduced into the district. It was made of cast iron, weighed 14lb less than the wooden ones, and cost £4 12s.

Go straight on through the gate and on downhill to Hepple.

A short distance along the road to the left at the edge of Hepple village is the ivy-covered ruin of the pele tower listed in 1415 as a Border fortress, and ruined by the Scots. It was probably built about 1350. Previous to the battle of Neville's Cross in 1346 when Edward III defeated the Scots, no vassal was allowed to erect a tower to fortify his dwelling in case he became too powerful. Here in the Borders, however, where there was constant harassment from the Scots, the rule was waived (and licence from the King not required). Most of the Border raids took place in moonlight during late autumn. Before turnips and modern feeding stuffs were introduced, it was not possible to over-winter many cattle, so the spare sheep and cattle were killed, salted and stored in a vault in the pele tower. The Reivers looked for grazing animals, not salted meat in store, so they set out to round up beasts before winter set in.

Turn right at the road and retrace your steps to the layby by the bridge.

Rothbury

Rothbury

Nestling in a wooded valley beside the River Coquet, this attractive little market town was called Routhebiria or Routha's town in the 12th century.

Three English monarchs have visited Rothbury. King John came to sign the town's charter in 1201; Edward I made a truce with the Scots in 1275 and sent the document from Rothbury, and Edward VII stayed at Cragside in 1884. The two earlier kings probably saw in 13th century Rothbury a collection of miserable mud hovels thatched with heather and straw or covered with grey stone slates. The last thatched house was demolished in 1891. Cock fighting and bull baiting were popular pastimes; in the 18th century there were no less than five cock pits in the town.

On the village green stood the covered, open-sided Market Cross; this was a useful building, erected in 1722, where men went to try on the new breeches they had a mind to purchase from the stalls, or sheltered from inclement weather. It was demolished in 1827. Nearby stood the pillory and stocks, the last occupant of the latter being Mr Archie Deedles who fell foul of the law in 1820, by being drunk and disorderly.

A new cross, made from stone quarried on the Cragside estate, was unveiled in 1902 to the memory of Lord and Lady Armstrong who died at the turn of the century.

The church, rebuilt, except for the 13th century chancel, has a most distinguished font comprising a carved shaft, part of a cross dating from about AD800, and a bowl of 1664.

Cragside, the old home of Lord Armstrong, and now belonging to the National Trust, with its romantic looking house and extensive wooded grounds, is on the outskirts of Rothbury.

Although the advent of the railway brought prosperity to Rothbury, that has now closed and even the bus service is infrequent.

Early closing day is Wednesday, but the National Park Information Centre, situated opposite the Green in the centre of Rothbury is open every day from Easter until the end of September.

8km about 3½ hours. This is a lovely walk offering extensive views. The going is easy; there are no steep hills to climb and the paths are clear, winding across a heather moor and through an attractive woodland.

Debdon road end is opposite the northern entrance to Cragside, about 2km north of Rothbury on the B6341; (GR 067034). Park carefully along the entrance road to Debdon, taking care not to obstruct the road or the driveway just to the right. Walk along the road, go through the gate and bear left downhill and over a little bridge to Primrose Cottage.

The predominant heather on this moor is ling *(Calluna vulgaris),* bearing pale purple flowers in spikes during late August and September. This plant has been used since Neolithic times for bedding, thatch, fuel, baskets, rope and brooms. An old English name for it was broom, and the word Calluna is derived from the Ancient Greek 'Kallona' meaning 'to cleanse' — presumably with a heather broom.

At the cottage turn right off the road through a gate, and walk beside the plantation (L) following the clear track.

Debdon Burn at Primrose Cottage

There is a fine wall, called a dry-stone dyke in Northumberland, running across the moor (R). Sandstone is the local rock and being reasonably soft it can be shaped, thus making a neater wall than can be crafted from the hard andesite rock of the Cheviot Hills. Dry-stone dyking is a very ancient, skilled craft and a very expensive undertaking today, costing about £15 a metre. Farmers will run a post and wire fence across their land rather than face that expense. In the National Park area, where the rebuilding of a stone dyke will enhance the scenic value of the countryside, the Park Authority usually pay part of the cost.

Go through the gate to a track crossroads. Continue in the same direction on the track through a wood and out onto open moorland.

This land was once part of the large Cragside estate, and the clear tracks were laid out as carriage drives used by the Armstrong family and their guests when out for an 'airing'.

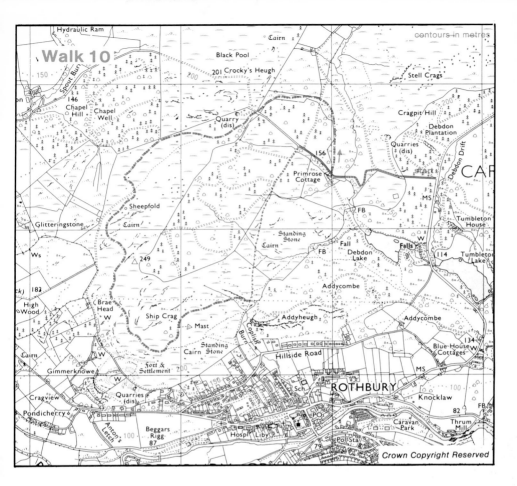

Cragside House and its immediate grounds now belong to the National Trust, but this tract of land still belongs to Lord Armstrong.

The track begins to curve round to the left, below the summit of the hill. Follow the track around the hill.

Away to the right lie the Cheviot Hills. The long hill is The Cheviot and to its right is Hedgehope. The red gash in the hillside is the Harden Quarry at Biddlestone, where red felsite is extracted. This attractive stone is used to surface roads and driveways.

On the right, too, not far from the foot of this high moor, can be seen the remains of Cartington Castle, beside the houses of the hamlet.

This 14th century castle gave lodging to Margaret, Queen of Scotland, and her infant daughter who was born a few miles away at Harbottle Castle in 1515. This baby grew up to become the mother of Lord Darnley, husband of Mary Queen of Scots. During the Civil War between Charles I and his Parliament, Roger Widdrington, then owner of the castle, espoused the cause of the King; after Roger's death his son Edward, fighting for the King at Marston Moor in 1644, was defeated by the Parliamentarians. As a result he was banished, his wife fined £400, a huge sum in those days, for giving intelligence to the King's party, and his estate sequestered. In 1648 the Parliamentary forces besieged the castle and after two hours it surrendered, badly damaged. Later it fell into decay and was abandoned.

55

Drystone wall and gateposts by the Carriage Drive

The track continues around another summit which is topped by a trig point.

Coquetdale lies below, and across the river rises the steep escarpment of the Simonside Hills. The big block of Simonside is flanked by Raven's Heugh to the right and Dover Crag to the left. Forestry Commission plantations clothe their slopes. These hills are part of the Fell Sandstone ridge which extends from the Kyloe Hills near Lowick, to the north-east, through Thrunton Crags and the Simonsides to some outcrops further west. This sandstone was laid down about 300 million years ago when large sandy deltas spread across the area. Later faulting and folding of the rocks produced steep escarpments all facing towards the Cheviots.

At a fork the track bears left and passes the tall TV aerial (R).

Grouse

This was erected in 1980 to improve programme reception for the town of Rothbury, tucked down in the valley and surrounded by hills. There are plenty of bilberries, also called blaeberries or whortleberries, to be found here, as they thrive on heathland. The delicious blue-black berries make fine tarts, but it takes a long time to gather a quantity. Sheep graze the shrub, keeping it low-growing, and birds like the fruit.

Continue on the track until 20m before a gate leads into a plantation. Turn left on a narrow path and follow it downhill over heather moor to a gate. Continue in the same direction, which after 400m leads to a stile in the angle of the plantation.

This is a good quality heather moorland, well suited to this type of soil. Grouse obviously love it and enjoy a good living from it judging by the numbers of plump little birds you will 'set up' on all sides as you walk along the narrow track.

About threequarters of the way along the track there is a small boundary stone with R marked on one side and D on the other. This is the boundary between Rothbury and Debden. Rothbury parish, an area of nearly 14,000 hectares, contained 2,545 people in 1851, to which Debden, one of its 28 townships, contributed 16 inhabitants.

Enter plantation by the path and then turn right along a forest track to a stile and T-junction. Turn right downhill to Primrose Cottage. Retrace your outward route on the road to the starting point.

9km, about 4 hours. An interesting, varied and reasonably level walk along quiet country roads, across fields, and passing by the historic cup and ring marked rock on Garleigh Moor. There is no clear path for the 500m across the moor, but Whittondean is in view.

Park at the Rothbury picnic site about 800m west of the town on the B6341 (GR 051016). Turn left out of the car park and walk along the road verge to a point just past the building (L) seen on the opposite bank of the river. Pass through the gate above the river and on down to the riverside. Bear right away from it to cross the ditches and stile in the fence seen ahead. Cross the field diagonally left to the footbridge.

This is Lady's Bridge. Perhaps it was given the name because it enabled ladies to cross the river and visit the woollen mills without risking the hazards of the ford. The Coquet used to be considered one of the finest fishing rivers in Northumberland and crowds of anglers were attracted to Rothbury. Some sources say the name Coquet is derived from the Celtic word 'coch' meaning red or peat-coloured water; others that it is a corruption of its 11th century name 'cocured' or cock's wood; apparently there were many game-cocks in its wooded valley.

Cross the bridge, bear left and follow the path (fence on left) which becomes a farm track leading to houses and metalled lane.

The once famous woollen mills stood here, well known for their Simonside plaids woven from the fleeces of upper Coquetdale sheep. The business was in the hands of one family for more than a century, but the secret of the manufacture of these special plaids died with the last member of the family to manage the mill.

Growing on the right hand side of the road is the dreaded bindweed, which can tangle itself and other plants into a solid mass. Great bindweed, with very large white, pink or stripey flowers, grows enthusiastically and anti-clockwise up the stay wire of a telegraph pole, twining a full circle up such a wire in $1\frac{1}{2}$-2 hours. As far back as 1548 it was recorded as a pestilential garden weed. The field bindweed, with smaller flowers, is a great spreader on bare, arable ground; in one

Path descent to Whittondean

Goldfinch

in every township, or cluster of farming communities, throughout the English Borders. When the watch raised the outcry by blowing of horns and shouting, every able man had to follow upon pain of death.

Pass East Newtown Farmhouse (the last building on the right), then turn right back into the farmyard. Turn immediately left through a gate in front of the farmhouse. Walk across the field on a track, bearing left to cross the Black Burn at the two large stone gateposts. Turn immediately right and walk on a raised bank (on old wall) to a fence. With the fence to your left walk up to a gate and continue beside the fence to the line of trees up left on the skyline. Walk alongside them.

season it has been known to cover 25m². Some country people call it withywind, others more plain speaking call it devil's guts.

Follow the lane uphill to a T-junction, then turn left on the road to Newtown.

The ruin of Great Tosson pele tower is seen to the right. This 15th century fortified house was more than necessary in an area such as Coquetdale, open to raiding by the Scots and the Reivers of Tynedale and Redesdale. In 1549 a range of warning beacons was established in the county, and in 1553 a complete system of 'watch and ward' was established

The creeping thistles in this field, with their fragrant lilac flowers on spineless stems, are weeds of cultivation. The many species of thistle are all members of the daisy family. The spear thistles *(Cirsium vulgare)* is also found in fields and is no friend to farmers, although goldfinches love its seeds and painted lady butterflies lay their eggs on the leaves; it has yellow-tipped spines beneath the pink-mauve flower. The musk thistle *(Carduus nutans)* is often found nodding its head on a spineless upper stalk. It has large purple spine-tipped bracts just behind the flower head. Where there is a bit of dampness the tall marsh thistle *(Cirsium palustre)* finds a home, usually with numerous purpley-red egg-shaped flowers.

Cup and Ring marked stones, Lordenshaw

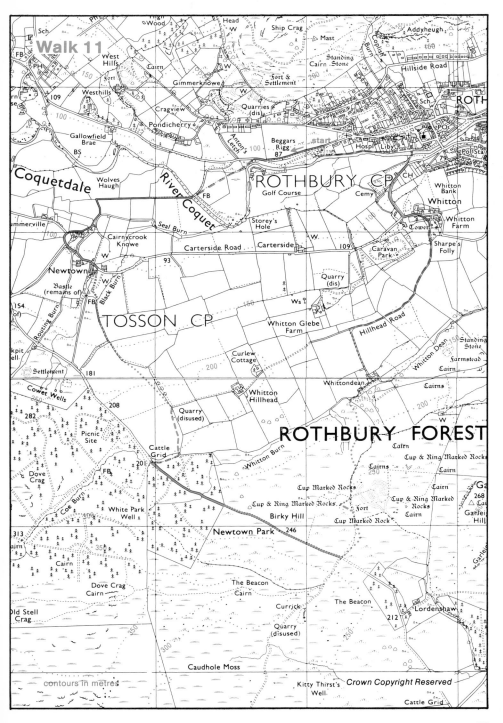

Walk 11

contours in metres

At the end of the trees walk beside the fence (L) to the plantation.

There is a small quarry on the right, the stone from which would have been used to build dykes and sheep stells.

Go through the gate, then another one on the right, and walk straight on along the clear path which soon leads to a road. Turn left.

The soil at the edge of the road is peaty and damp, so cross-leaved heath is to be found with its compact heads of pink flowers. It gets its name from the way the narrow linear leaves are formed in a cross on the stem. It is popular with bees, who also like the self-heal found here beside it. Self-heal, with tiny blossoms of rich purple, is widespread and blooms all summer. It was formerly credited with wonderful curative powers and was used to heal all manner of ills.

Walk along the road.

The trees here are Norway spruce, the Christmas tree, and Sitka spruce which has a bluish appearance due to two bright blue-white bands beneath each leaf. The larch has a bedraggled look in winter when its leaves have fallen, (it is one of the very few deciduous conifers), but in spring the young leaves are a beautiful pale green. Wordsworth, the Lakeland poet, didn't like this colour: he thought it out of keeping with the countryside. Larch was introduced into England in the 16th century and the first grown as an ornamental tree, but later used for its valuable timber. More varieties were planted in the 18th century, and now Japanese larch is the one most often found in plantations and on reclaimed mine tips.

Adder

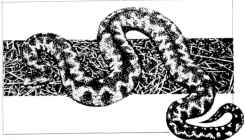

Follow road up the slope to the open moorland.

The Simonside Hills rear to the right. The name is said to be derived from Sigemund's Seat or settlement. In 1279 the name was Simundessete. On the top of the hills is a lonely moor of which many tales were told long ago, with mischievous elves luring folk into bogs or over the crags.

About 200m before the road reaches a plantation turn left at the waymark and walk straight across the moor for a short distance to a gate. Now bear slightly left, along a clear grassy track. Near the top of the slope another path leads up left to a large sandstone rock.

A large sandstone block lies just to the left of the path. Carved into it are a number of hollows surrounded by channels. These are called cup and ring markings and date from the Bronze Age. Their meaning is lost in the mists of antiquity, but because stones with these markings have been found in burial sites, it is thought they may have had a religious significance. This moor has many prehistoric burial grounds, a 'camp' and a stone alignment; the latter, an avenue of small standing stones, was possibly of sacred significance to people of that period. In early times it must have been a place of some importance.

A hundred years ago or so pitmen, working the local drift mines, used to bring their beehives to the moor during July and August for the heather blossom. It is said that up to a thousand hives would be put here for the summer.

From the rock return to the grassy track. Turn left and walk on in the same direction as before (do not walk to the top of the hill). In a short distance a grassy area is seen. Just before it, turn right through bracken to follow a ruined stone wall downhill until a sunken track crosses it at some hawthorn trees. Turn left and descend to the bottom left hand corner of the woodland seen below, with Whittondean Houses beside it.

Bracken can be a nuisance on the hills, but is not easily eliminated. It smothers the grass

Sharp's Folly

and in early autumn is poisonous to cattle, so they have to be removed from it. The adder, or viper, our only poisonous snake, often hides in bracken, so when it is tall in summer try and follow a sheep track where the ground is visible.

At the bottom corner of the plantation, go through the gate.

It is worth pausing a moment by the pond; a little world in itself it is an example of a wildlife habitat that has decreased because of land drainage and now a rare sight in many parts of England. Creatures that rely on ponds, like frogs and dragonflies, have disappeared too and it is good to see that this one still has a healthy population of both aquatic creatures and the plants on which they depend. Water-boatmen sometimes seem to outnumber the other invertebrates, and since the great water-boatman *(Notonecta)* is a voracious predator there is a danger that at these times the pond might be 'cleaned out' of stock, whereupon the boatmen fly off to other ponds and start the process again.

61

Pass the pond (L) and walk ahead for 50m. Turn left along a track leading up the slope passing in front of the cottages.

A dene, or dean, is a narrow wooded valley, like the one seen ahead, from which Whitton-dean takes its name.

Follow the track by turning left through the farm garden (waymarked) to continue along the farm road to a junction. Turn right and go along the lane.

The hedgerows here are full of wild flowers, as all hedgerows were before the advent of spraying and verge cutting. Meadow cranesbill *(Geranium pratense)* likes grassy places where there is a bit of lime; the big five-petalled blue flowers make a striking show. Tufted vetch, a member of the pea family, clambers among stronger stemmed plants which give it support. The spikes of its blue-violet flowers make a show all summer long. Lady's bedstraw favours dry banks like the ones along this lane, and has bright yellow flowers in leafy clusters. One of its names is cheese rennet, from a former use of the flowers to curdle milk in cheese making. It has also been used as a dye, and it is said that if animals feed upon it their bones are reddened.

In Chaucer's time beds were made of straw and bedstraw, and according to legend lady's bedstraw was used with bracken as bedding in Christ's manger.

Walk along the lane to the trees and a ruined stone tower.

Among the trees, by the roadside (L) is Sharp's Folly. This round tower was built by Thomas Sharp, a local rector from 1720 to 1758. It was primarily relief work for the unemployed, but Sharp, who practised astrology, used it as an observatory. Before the trees grew around it, the sea was visible from the top.

Follow the track past the tower bearing left

at the fork and onto the road. Turn left to walk downhill to a road junction.

On the left at the crossroads is Whitton Tower, standing back in its grounds. This was originally a 14th century pele tower, but it was repaired and added to, becoming a rectory and later a children's convalescent home.

Turn right, downhill, for a short distance past the cemetery, then walk across the car park (L) and the footbridge.

This riverside recreation area is a popular spot.

Turn left and walk upstream beside the River Coquet until the houses seen above you end.

Just beside the garden wall of the large house on the right grows a plant which likes a waterside environment. This is comfrey, which being tall is easily seen. The creamy white or mauve bell-like flowers in curving forked clusters are quite distinctive. Long ago plants had local or colloquial names which varied not only from county to county but almost from village to village, causing great confusion among serious scientists. But in the 18th century this changed when a Swedish botanist called Car Von Linne (Linnaeus) devised a new binomial system, which has served us well ever since. Each plant is given generic or a 'surname', starting with a capital letter which describes the group or genus to which the plant is closely related. This is followed by a specific name, not starting with a capital letter, which describes the individual species. The combination of names 'latinised' into a standard language, is unique and enables botanists from different countries to converse in confidence.

A few metres further on, turn right up the bank partially stepped to the picnic site. Turn left through the site then up more steps (R) to the car park.

River bank beyond Elyhaugh ▶

THE COQUETDALE RIVER WALK

The Coquetdale River Walk: Rothbury - Felton

This long river walk begins at Rothbury and ends at Felton, 22km of varied river, wood and farmland landscape along the middle reaches of an outstanding Northumbrian valley.

From its source high in the Cheviots at Coquethead on the English-Scottish border, the River Coquet cuts a deep, zigzag course through uplands of bleached grass and heather moorland until it reaches the village of Alwinton. From here it meanders gently through rolling pasture and scattered woodlands across the broad vale of Coquetdale. To the north are the Cheviot Hills whilst to the south lie the craggy outcrops of the Simonsides, part of the ancient forest of Rothbury. At last the river emerges onto the broad coastal plain to enter the sea at the historic town of Warkworth.

Largely as a result of its meandering lower course the Coquet has the distinction of being the longest river in Northumberland, extending to 88km. One quarter of its length is described here in a linear walk beginning at Rothbury and ending at Felton. The route, despite being 22km long, is an easy one, having no long climbs, although there are several short steep pulls up the high river bank. For connoisseurs of gradient there is the built-in advantage of following this river

Ash tree on Thornyhaugh track

downstream. Walk suitably shod as the paths beside the river are often muddy and slippery and grass pastures may be long and wet. Use stiles to avoid opening gates, and please keep dogs on a lead at all times.

The Coquetdale walk can be done in one long day or divided into three easy outings for all the family. Whichever way it is tackled, there is reward in its accomplishment as a big walk following the most natural scenic route through some of the best of lowland Northumberland.

Cross the River Coquet by the bridge in Rothbury (GR 058016) to walk southwards up the B6342 Hexham road for 400m.

Rothbury bridge dates back to about the 16th century; its was originally a narrow one for pack horses.

The old Corn Road from Hexham to Alnmouth passed this way. During the 18th century particularly, many open fields and common lands were enclosed and there were improve-

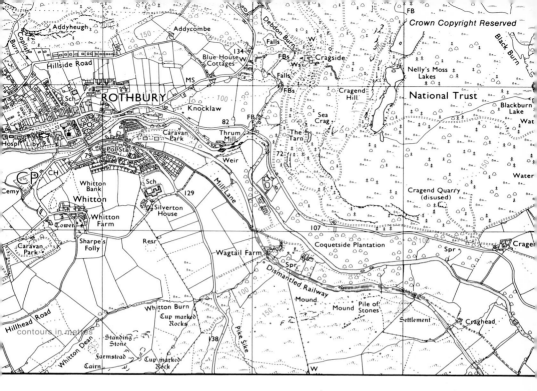

contours in metres

ments in agricultural methods; new crop rotations were introduced, such as turnips and grass which broke the sequence of corn crops, yet did away with the need to leave land fallow and out of use. More corn was needed; the population was increasing and merchant ships leaving for the colonies had to be provisioned. Successive governments, from as early as Charles II's reign, promoted increased production of corn by banning imported grain and at the same time offering the English farmer bounties for its export. These Corn Laws began to have their full effect in the 18th century. The major problem came when they had to transport the corn from the field to the point of sale. Roads everywhere in England were appalling — little more than tracks, rutted by the wheels of large wagons and often impassable in winter.

Alnmouth was a flourishing port and well able to handle grain, so in 1753/4 a road from Hexham to Alnmouth via Rothbury and Alnwick was constructed. This Corn Road, 44 miles long, necessitated the building of 5 bridges and a number of turnpikes, and was estimated

to cost £4,400. From here the Corn Road went on past the entrance to Cragside and uphill across the moors to Alnwick.

Rothbury bridge had to be widened in 1759 to accommodate the wagons, and again in the early 20th century.

Take the left hand road (marked 'No Through Road') and walk beside the houses (R) and continue until just before reaching a bridge.

The houses are soon left behind and one walks along the lane where, in season, wild roses make a splash of colour in the hedges. The Ancient Greeks used rose petals for perfume and even for carpeting. People used to think that God created diseases, but also created cures in flowers, and gave each a 'signature' as a clue to its potential value. The thorn of a rose was thought to resemble a dog's tooth so the root of the plant was used to heal dog bites; hence one possible explanation for the name dog rose (Rosa canina). Sometimes one sees a gall, or swelling on the dog rose. This is called robin's pincushion, or

65

briar ball, and is caused by the quite small gall wasp. The gall is closely covered by long, branched reddish hairs and is brightly coloured. It matures in May on the twigs and leaves of wild roses and then the adult gall wasp emerges. The females lay their eggs in the plant tissues and these stimulate the plant into producing the galls. Apothecaries used to powder the galls from which they made a drink to cure colic. If the grubs were found inside the gall, that was a welcome extra, to be dried and powdered and made into another drink for the cure of worms in the belly.

Much smaller and lower down on the bank are the white starry flowers of greater stitch-wort, often called White Sunday because its flowers appeared at the time of White or Low Sunday, six weeks before Whit Sunday.

Follow the road down left and under the bridge and on for 100m.

This railway branch line which ran from Scots Gap to Rothbury opened in 1870 and put Rothbury on the map. The line ran through pretty countryside and the gentle run down the wooded slopes to the little village of Rothbury, nestling among the hills, was considered quite spectacular. Visitors flocked there and it began to develop and expand. The line, like so many others, was closed in 1963, but the visitors still come by car.

Where the road bends left to Wagtail Farm go straight on through a gate on the track.

Grey wagtail

If Wagtail Farm was named after a bird, it was probably the beautiful grey wagtail. This colourful bird is fond of rocky streams, liking to build its nest in a hole in the bank. It has a noticeable long black tail with conspicuous white outer feathers, blue-grey upper parts and yellow under the tail.

The pied wagtail, black and white and with a very bouncy tail also likes the waterside, but is frequently seen in fields and on lawns. Pied wagtails seem to have a particular liking for greenhouses in which they will often roost, in winter. In the breeding season the males are aggressive and will fight each other as well as their reflections in mirrors, windows and even the hub caps of cars.

Go through another gate and continue on the track for 800m to a railway cutting through rock.

This part of the valley with its old, gnarled trees harbouring a multitude of insects beneath the bark, is the haunt of the great spotted woodpecker, another beautiful bird more often heard than seen. A sudden loud drumming betrays its presence. The rattling sound is made by an extremely rapid series of blows with the bill upon tree boughs. Although it is a colourful bird with a black back, large white shoulder patches and crimson under the tail and the male has a crimson patch on the back of its head, it seems to be well camouflaged in the woodland and is hard to see. Great spotted woodpeckers are fond of nuts and will visit bird tables in winter.

Continue on the track through a gate and after 50m turn left through another gate into a field. Go right, across the field to pass to the right of Crag Head cottage via a gate.

This is one of the many abandoned farm cottages to be seen on and around the Cheviot Hills. Four hundred years ago they were abandoned because of harassment by the Scottish Border Reivers; now it is because farm mechanisation has made many agricultural workers redundant.

Follow the track across six fields (with gates) to West Row farmyard.

At the farm, notice the open circular shed with a slate roof. This would have been a 'gin-gan' or horse wheel shed. 'Gin' is short for engine and 'gan' is a dialect word meaning 'to go'. Horses harnessed to a wheel paced around to produce power which drove a threshing machine in the adjoining barn.

Longhaugh from Thornyhaugh track

Turn right at the farm buildings, and walk through the gate to a T-junction. Turn right and walk to a road junction, and then almost immediately go through the gate (L) and cross the field (fence on your left) passing to the right of the cottage. Just past the cottage are two gates. Go through the right-hand one and on by a fence (L) for 100m to go through the second gate on the left. Then turn right following the fence and later the big hedge (R) to just before the end of field. Curve round left and after 100m go through a wicket gate and down through the plantation to another wicket gate.

The loud clattering whirr of a rising cock pheasant is likely to be heard in plantations such as this. Gamebirds, and many others that live in woods have short, rounded wings, and in general have stout as well as short quills, which is why they make more noise at the start of a flight when the wings are moved very rapidly, in order to take off in the confined space of a wood.

The pheasant is not native to the British Isles; it is thought to have been introduced into the country by the Romans. Later, varieties such as the ring-necked pheasant from East China were brought over here, so that the birds of today are usually hybrids. For all that, the male pheasant is a very smart looking bird, albeit rather aggressive towards other cock pheasants in the breeding season when feathers may fly in all directions.

Continue beside a sike to cross the little bridge (R) and walk on left around the field above the River Coquet to a gate. Cross the next field directly to a gate to the right of Pauperhaugh Bridge.

Pauperhaugh, called locally Popperhoff, was originally named Papwirthalge. The bridge is scheduled as of special architectural and historic interest. There is no mention of it in early county records, so it was probably built in the 19th century as a private bridge.

Great spotted woodpeckers

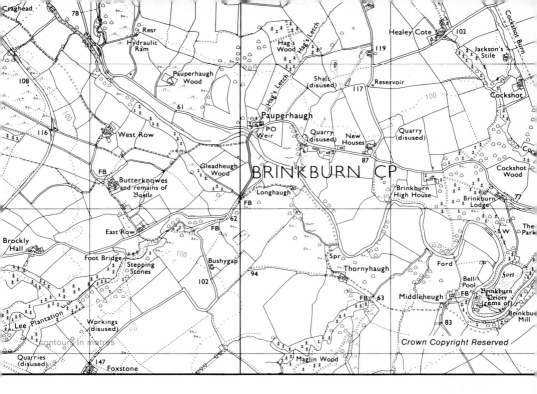

Crown Copyright Reserved

contours in metres

Turn right and walk southwards from the bridge (GR 100995) with your back to the river, for 400m along the road.

A glance at all the debris caught up in the hedges is a reminder that after prolonged rain or heavy snowfall the Coquet overflows its banks and this road becomes impassable.

Watch carefully for the small footbridge (L) over the forest burn. Cross it, turn left, and walk a few metres around the low hill. Then go over the stile and with the fence to your right walk on to pass to the left of Longhaugh Cottage. Turn left now to walk downstream beside the River Coquet.

Willow trees, lovers of the waterside, grow along the river banks. There are some 300 species of willow, 19 of them native to Britain, and ranging in size from trees to small shrubs. A variety of the white willow provides wood for making cricket bats. Another species, the common osier, is often pollarded — the crown is cut bodily away at a point about 5m above the ground. The trunk then puts out

masses of slender branches, and their multitudinous twigs — often spoken of as osiers —are used in basket making.

At the field end turn right and walk beside the sike for 50m to the gate and small bridge at the foot of a track.

Great willowherb grows in this damp spot; its popular name is codlins and cream.

This is our tallest and largest-flowered willowherb, growing 90-180cm high; its purplish pink flowers bloom throughout the summer. There are four petals and a long, narrow stalk-like ovary which bursts open late in the season to allow the escape of cottony seeds which are wafted away in the wind.

Walk up the track, passing just to the right of Thornyhaugh farmhouse to a track junction. Turn left and follow the track for 50m to turn right around the farmhouse wall and go through the gate. With the fence to your right, walk across the field and down to the footbridge over the Maglin Burn.

69

Longhaugh and Thornyhaugh were part of Rothbury Forest. The word 'forest' did not necessarily mean a fully treed area, but a hunting ground. In 1204 King John granted the hunting rights to Robert son of Roger. Hunting without his permit resulted in a fine of £10 in silver and the forfeit of horses, harness and dogs: a very heavy fine indeed, in those days.

In the 18th century much of the Forest was enclosed, but there still remained many of the bastle houses constructed of 1½m thick walls with loophole windows and a vaulted lower floor to accommodate cattle. In the 16th and 17th centuries this area suffered much from the Border raids, the Scottish Reivers, or robbers, riding down to steal cattle and anything else they fancied.

All those old bastles, or fortified houses, have now vanished, but Bushy Gap, a farmhouse just along the road from Thornyhaugh, still has a touch of romance. In the 18th century there was much smuggling of liquor in upper Coquetdale; Scotch whisky came in kegs on horse-back over the Cheviots, and gin was brought from Boulmer on the coast. The farmer at Bushy Gap kept three swift horses for this trade, and a local rhyme ran:—

Awd Bob Dunn o' the Forest,
He's three fam'd horses
Fra' Bushy Gap lonnin',
But 'Kate of the West is queen o' them aa'.
The farmhouse had a double gable and in this space the gin was hidden. It was a long time before this secret hiding place was discovered and the farmer brought to justice and heavily fined.

Cross the bridge and walk up the slope —bearing slightly left across the field to a gate.

Many wild flowers grow on this bank. The tiny eyebright has small, but very beautiful white flowers with purple streaks and a spot of yellow. The plant is a partial parasite; it manufactures some chlorophyll but not sufficient for its needs, so it relies upon the roots of grasses for much of its food. It was used by herbalists in the treatment of eye troubles.

Another interesting plant to be seen here is devil's bit scabious. It carries rounded heads of dark blue flowers in late summer. Culpeper, the herbalist, said it was excellent for curing the plague, fever and freckles! Somewhere along the line it upset the Devil who took revenge by biting off the end of the tap root, hence its name. Slopes like this, difficult to plough and re-seed, carry the interesting and lovely wild flowers which years ago were to be found in every pasture and hedgerow.

Bear left across the field in the direction of the farm building. Go through a wicket gate in the fence and diagonally left across a small field to the road. Cross the road and the stile opposite. Turn left and follow the burn, then a plantation fence, up left around the field to the top of the plantation.

Coquetdale has ever been famous for the longevity of its inhabitants. Middleheugh was farmed in the first half of the 18th century by Henry Collingwood, who lived for more than a hundred years. He retained his senses to the last and died greatly beloved in the neighbourhood.

At the top of the field go through a wicket gate and walk above the tree covered cliff (fence on left).

Devil's bit scabious

Pauperhaugh Bridge ▶

The River Coquet can be heard as it tumbles over the rocks below, making a great loop around Brinkburn Priory. In high summer the foliage obscures the view a little, but the Priory is in a very beautiful spot. It was founded in the 12th century for Augustinian Canons, the first Prior coming from Pentney Priory in Norfolk, to which Brinkburn remained subordinate until late in the 12th century. In 1536 it was suppressed with other lesser monasteries, its income amounting to only £69 per annum, and passed into lay hands.

There are many tales about Brinkburn. It suffered much from Scottish raids, and tradition says that on one occasion the Scots missed the Priory, concealed as it was among the trees, and were returning home when they heard the pealing of its bells, rung by the monks in thanksgiving for their deliverence. Needless to say the Scots turned round and galloped back to deal out fire and slaughter to the valley.

Some time later, in 1717, a band of tinkers who were roaming the area made off with the chapel bell.

In 1834 a labourer, shovelling away debris from a burned-out wooden building near the church remarked of a certain shovelful that it was the heaviest he had ever handled. To the surprise of the workmen, it was found to contain a brass pot full of gold coins from the reigns of Edward III and Richard II.

The church remained in use until 1683, then fell into decay, but the Cadogan family who owned the estate commissioned the Newcastle architect Thomas Austin to draw up plans for its restoration in 1857. This was accomplished most successfully and the church, now in the hands of the English Heritage Commission, is open to the public. Some say the church is haunted, but that only adds to its interest and charm. J.M.W. Turner painted Brinkburn when it was a forlorn ruin.

Brinkburn Priory

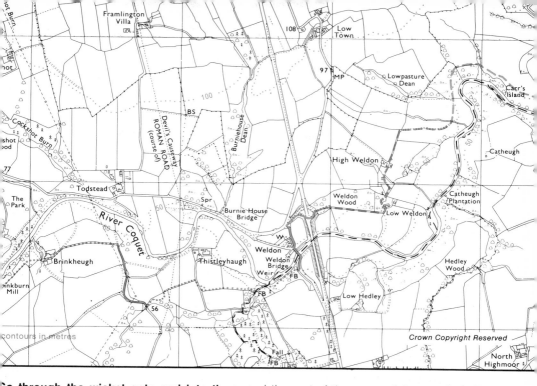

Go through the wicket gate and into the field, following the path beside the trees (L) to the end of the field. Turn right beside the fence and go through a gate (L) and walk on to the farm.

The names of the farms passed at the beginning of this walk ended in 'haugh', now they end in 'heugh'. This seems confusing, apart from the pronunciation, 'haugh' sounding rather like 'hurf' and 'heugh' like 'heuf'.

Both these words derive from Old English. Haugh means flat land by a stream and heugh means a projecting ridge which ends abruptly. So, in reality, the farms are correctly named according to their position.

At Brinkheugh Farm go through a gate and pass between the buildings, down the track to a metalled lane. Continue down the lane.

To the left is the hamlet of Todstead where on 5 June 1833 a swarm of bees alighted on the head of Mrs Gibb. The lady was said to have been 'a little alarmed', but a resourceful spectator removed the queen bee to a hive

and the rest of the swarm followed without inflicting a single sting upon poor Mrs Gibb.

Follow the lane, passing the drive to Thistley-haugh (L) and continue to a road junction. Turn left along the road for 250m towards a bridge. Just before the bridge go through a gate on the left. Walk up the slope on a track above the burn and turn left to a white gate in the fence on the left. Turn right and walk beside the fence and hedge (R).

A few yards into the field the path crosses the course of the Devil's Causeway. This Roman road was a branch of Watling Street and ran in an almost straight line from Hadrian's Wall near Hexham to the mouth of the Tweed.

At the lane turn right for a few metres, then enter the field just right of the ruined cottage. Follow the hedge (R) across the fields and down the slope alongside a wood to the footbridge over the Tod Burn. Turn left by a fence in the woodland to follow the path by the River Coquet. Continue to a little foot-bridge leading onto road and turn left. Walk over the bridge and up past the Angler's

Arms to a road junction. Turn right and walk through the underpass.

Weldon Bridge dates from 1744. It has had a chequered history, having been damaged many times by floods and by having its stones displaced as huge horse wagons, and later motor lorries, tried to negotiate it. The 19th century mail coaches on the Newcastle to Edinburgh run called at the Angler's Arms.

Weldon Bridge and its Inn have been well-known to the fishing fraternity for hundreds of years. In days gone by the river was full of large trout and salmon, and there was, of course, a great deal of poaching. Local people were wont to say that their year's rent to the landlord lay in the Coquet.

Many angling songs and poems have been written about the sport to be had in the Coquet and the hospitality offered by the Inn. Here is a verse from one of them:

At Weldon Bridge ther's wale o' wine
If ye hae coin in pocket,
If ye can thraw a heckle fine,
Ther's wale o' trout in Coquet.

Take the farm road leading eastwards 50m from the end of the underpass. If you are beginning the walk at this point then the start is the underpass to Brinkburn on the eastern side of the A697 road bridge over the River Coquet (GR 138988).

The new road bridge was opened in 1969 This road used to be a turnpike highway along which bowled horse drawn carriages of every description. Perhaps the most romantic was the mail coach which made a stop at the Angler's Arms, Weldon Bridge. Mail coaches were introduced in 1784 and though they ran for little more than 60 years no other period of horse drawn traffic has so fired the imagination. Post boys — young or old — who earlier had carried the post, now met the coach and took mail on horseback down the byroads.

Weir above Weldon Bridge

Middleheugh

The mail coaches, travelling as they did throughout the night, were subject to many dangers. A traveller at the time wrote 'Give me a collision, a broken axle and an overturn, a runaway team, a drunken coachman, snow-storms, howling tempests, but Heaven preserve us from floods!'.

On the other hand, mail coaches could be a danger to other road users. Lit by up to five lamps and often drawn by loaned tempestuous carriage horses to 'calm them down', these radiant swiftnesses hurtling along the roads at a pace considerably over ten miles an hour were quite frightening to meet. Many a coach-man blinded by the glare and alarmed by the thundering of the hooves feared a collision and promptly drove into the ditch as being the lesser of two evils.

The roads were often rutted and pot-holed. An Act of Parliament in 1555 made the Parish responsible for their upkeep, but the grudged labour and inefficient method of road repair led to the setting up of Turnpike Trusts in the 17th century. The public invested money in bonds and were to be paid interest from the sums collected from road users at tollgates. However, although the Post Office sent officials to inspect the roads and heavy fines were inflicted upon Parishes whose roads were neglected, the mail coaches paid no tolls. Woe betide any tollgate keeper who, upon hearing the Tantivy blown on the posthorn by the armed guard, did not immediately throw open the gate and let the mail coach rush through, for free!

This loss of revenue was considerable and finally the Turnpike Acts lapsed and the system was abandoned and many investors lost all their money.

The stretch of road here at Weldon Bridge was none too safe. In 1772 and 1773 there were complaints of footpads and mounted highwaymen attacking travellers. On one occasion a woman was robbed, and another

75

time the driver of the Newcastle to Edinburgh Fly was held up and robbed of five shillings and tuppence. However, the highwayman returned him the tuppence so that he could get through the tollgate.

Follow the road, soon a track, passing to the left of Low Weldon Farm. Walk uphill and at High Weldon go straight on along the track which after a short distance turns right through a gate and continues to another gate beside the trees. Go through this, cross the small field and leaving the track, bear left through a gate uphill on a path skirting the bracken. Go through another gate (R) and walk above the trees (R) and the River Coquet. At the end of the field go through the wicket gate across the small burn.

Flood-water on the Coquet near Weldon Bridge

Herons fish the river and are often seen standing quietly in the shallows, or flying overhead. They feed largely on fish but are not averse to rats, ducklings or any other small creature they can kill with their formidable bill. Herons nest for the most part high up in tall trees, but they no longer breed in this area. Long ago these birds ranked among royal game and were protected as such by law; whoever destroyed their eggs was liable to the then large penalty of 20 shillings for each offence. Heron hawking was a favourite diversion among the nobility at whose tables the bird was an esteemed dish.

From the wicket gate continue along the right-hand edge of field to another wicket. Go through this, bear right and continue beside the trees and over a stile. From the

stile bear left along a ridge in the field to a gate 400m ahead. Continue, fence on your right, to cross a stile at the field end. Continue straight across the field to a gate left of Elyhaugh. Cross the track and through another gate to turn right past the house by a burn.

This house at Elyhaugh is dated 1732 and has rather unusual stonework above the windows and door facing the river. It was built by Thomas Lisle whose family had lived at Elyhaugh since 1549.

Walk 50m and go through a gate by the River Coquet to walk close by the river to a fence. Turn left through wicket gates and continue a little left, (slightly away from the river) across a field until the river is reached again by a bridged sike. Follow the path uphill above the river to a gate, up through the gate, and bear right on a narrow path to cross the footbridge over the burn. Continue above the trees and River Coquet to a big footbridge across Swarland Burn.

St. Michael's Church, Felton

Alders line the river bank; like willows they thrive best close to a waterside site. Alders are unusual in that they have stalked buds, and the leaves, instead of tapering towards the tip, are broader at that end than the other. When alders are cut, the wood, although conspicuously white at first, soon assumes a red colour when exposed to the air. The woody seed cases, like little fir cones, are noticeable on the bare boughs of winter.

Cross the footbridge. There are local walks waymarked in this woodland so take care to turn right for a short distance, then left and onto a woodland path above the river. After 50m a track is reached, turn right and follow it for 1km to the underpass.

This path above the Coquet follows the Mill Banks, and to the left the tree-covered area is called Tile Kiln Rush and behind it is the Kiln Field. These names indicate that in the days when communities were self-supporting there was a corn mill hereabouts driven by water power from the Coquet, and a tilery making clay roof tiles and drainage pipes.

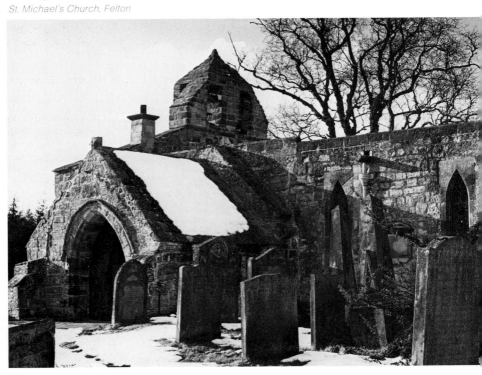

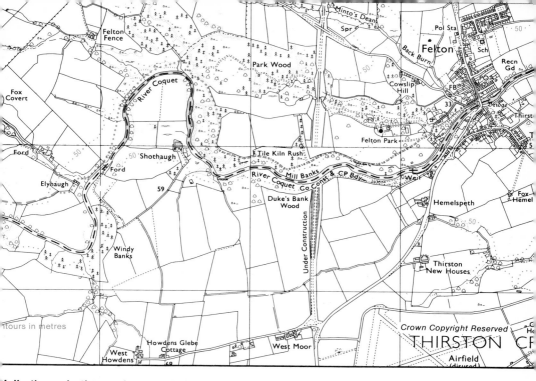

Crown Copyright Reserved

THIRSTON CF

Walk through the underpass below the road.

For many years the A1 road carried an ever increasing traffic volume through Felton village. Finally, after nearly half a century's battle with the authorities, the villagers saw his bypass opened in 1981.

Follow the path above the River Coquet to wicket gate. Continue across field, bearing slightly left away from river to the stretch of tarmac which leads to a wicket gate and the road.

St Michael's is an interesting and unusual looking church, with its low roof over nave and aisle. It dates in part from the early 13th century; the massive porch is 15th century, but the extraordinarily heavy bellcote is of a later date. Although Felton seems far from Scotland the Scottish Reivers rode this way and armies marched to and fro. During restorations in 1870 seventy skulls were found lying together, also a number of spurs and Scottish coins — the sad relics of some long forgotten raid or battle.

In 1303 Edward I visited Felton and graciously made a donation of seven shillings towards the upkeep of the church.

With the church to your left walk down the hill.

Felton, situated as it is on fairly level ground between the Cheviots and the sea, which made for an easy route to Scotland, has seen much history. Here, in 1215, the Northumbrian barons transferred their allegiance from King John to Alexander, King of Scots. John was not exactly pleased and the following year ordered Felton to be burnt down.

In 1291 Edward I passed through on his way to Berwick upon Tweed to settle a dispute. Alexander, King of Scots, had fallen over a cliff and his grand-daughter, Margaret of Norway had died on her way to Scotland, so Edward I rode up to choose a successor. Robert Bruce and John Balliol were the chief claimants; Edward chose John and then demanded recognition as overlord of Scotland, thus starting the 300 years of bloodshed and misery known as the Border Troubles.

79

In 1314 Edward II visited the village after his defeat by Robert Bruce at Bannockburn in Scotland; he was back again in 1322.

The Duke of Cumberland and his army rested at Felton before going on to fight the Young Pretender, Charles Stuart, at Culloden in 1746. Mr Edward Widdrington, a local land-owner, caused the contents of his cellar to be carted to the village street and the soldiers were regaled with beef, bread and beer. The Duke was well pleased, but Mr Widdrington said that although he wished the Duke's family well, he detested internal commotions as neither plenty nor pleasure could be enjoyed independent of peace.

A person less well pleased with the village was John Wesley who, while on a missionary tour in 1766, gave a stirring address to the assembled populace, but wrote in his journal that 'very few seemed to understand anything of the matter'.

At the junction turn right for the village and the end of the walk.

Felton Old Bridge, seen to the right, is sched-uled as an 'Ancient Monument', being one of the few medieval bridges still standing on the Coquet. It was mentioned in 1562 when the passage between Thistleyhaugh and Newton-on-the-Moor had to be watched nightly against marauding Scots.

The bridge narrowly missed destruction during the 17th century Civil War, when Sir Thomas Glenham proposed its demolition in order to hamper the movement of opposing armies.

◀ *Coquet from Felton Bridge*

Glossary

Bastle

A fortified farmhouse, with thick walls and small windows. The family lived on the first floor and the cattle were kept on the ground floor. Bastle houses date from the 16th century.

Burn

A small river or stream.

Cairn

A heap of stones to mark a pathway, or indicate a prehistoric burial site.

Cleugh

A ravine, pronounced 'cluff'.

Dyke

A wall.

Haugh

Flat land by a burn.

Heugh

A hill which ends abruptly.

Hope

A strip of fertile land in a narrow valley.

Knowe

A small hill or moorland slope.

Law

A hill.

Pele

A fortified tower house, 14th-17th century lived in by vicars and lesser gentry.

Reiver

Robber.

Shiel

A summer grazing ground, or the simple huts used on such a ground.

Sike

A very small burn.

Stell

A circular enclosure of stone, used for sheltering sheep.

Tor

A large outcrop of rock, harder than the surrounding rock and thus more resistant to erosion.

For Further Reading

THE STEEL BONNETS
by G. McDonald Fraser
Pan Books, 1974

LIFE AND DEATH IN PREHISTORIC NORTHUMBERLAND
by Stan Beckensall
Frank Graham, 1976

ROCKS AND SCENERY FROM TYNE TO TWEED
by G.R. Warn
Frank Graham, 1975

NORTHUMBERLAND — NATIONAL PARK GUIDE NO. 7
Edited by J. Philipson
H.M.S.O., 1969

RIVER BRIDGES OF NORTHUMBERLAND VOL. II, THE COQUET
by T. Dickens
from Brands Books, High Street, Wooler

NORTHUMBRIAN CASTLES, WANSBECK AND COQUET
Frank Graham, 1974

A CORNER IN THE NORTH
(YESTERDAY AND TODAY WITH BORDER FOLK)
A book about old customs by H. Neville
Frank Graham, reprinted 1980

Northumberland National Park
and Countryside Publications

The publications listed here may be purchased from all good
booksellers in the north-east and from National Park, or Country Park Information Centres

WALKS IN THE HADRIAN'S WALL AREA

WALKS ON THE NORTHUMBERLAND COAST

WALKS IN THE CHEVIOT HILLS

THE STORY OF REDESDALE

LOOK AROUND HADRIAN'S WALL AREA

THE CHEVIOT WAY OF LIFE
Available 1986

A FIELD GUIDE TO THE HADRIAN'S WALL AREA

A FIELD GUIDE TO PLESSEY WOODS

A FIELD GUIDE TO THE CHEVIOT HILLS

Further titles in this series are planned or in preparation

If difficulty is experienced in obtaining copies please write to the address below.

For general information about Northumberland National Park write (SAE please) to
The National Park Officer, Eastburn, South Park, Hexham, Northumberland, NE46 1BS

Comments and suggestions relating to this publication are welcomed.